Provision Mapping and the SEND Code of Practice

In the busy world that schools inhabit, this book provides clear guidance on how to implement a simple and user-friendly system that will ensure all pupil progress is forensically examined and any inadequacies swiftly addressed. *Provision Mapping and the SEND Code of Practice* describes a tried and tested system that helps schools to successfully identify, implement and track provision for all pupils, irrespective of whether they have a special educational need or not.

This new edition:

- demonstrates how schools can implement the requirements of the new SEND Code of Practice
- provides achievable solutions to the problems that schools face in trying to evidence the impact of the additional support they provide
- provides reproduceable templates of tables that can be used to track progress of all pupils
- contains easy to use tools that will allow a school to clearly evidence that additional funding is used efficiently.

This second edition has been fully updated to reflect the recent changes to SEN legislation, the new SEND Code of Practice (2015), the new National Curriculum and new assessment requirements and the new Common Inspection Framework. Additional material has been added to provide a resource for secondary and special schools. Headteachers, senior managers, leadership teams, SENCOs and other educational professionals will find the guidance and support provided by this book invaluable.

Anne Massey is an experienced SENCO and school leader, now working as an independent consultant with schools and local authorities across the UK.

nasen is a professional membership association that supports all those who work with or care for children and young people with special and additional educational needs. Members include teachers, teaching assistants, support workers, other educationalists, students and parents.

nasen supports its members through policy documents, journals, its magazine *Special*, publications, professional development courses, regional networks and newsletters. Its website contains more current information such as responses to government consultations. nasen's published documents are held in very high regard both in the UK and internationally.

Other titles published in association with the National Association for Special Educational Needs (nasen):

Language for Learning in the Secondary School: A practical guide for supporting students with speech, language and communication needs
Sue Hayden and Emma Jordan
2012/pb: 978-0-415-61975-2

Using Playful Practice to Communicate with Special Children
Margaret Corke
2012/pb: 978-0-415-68767-6

The Equality Act for Educational Professionals: A simple guide to disability and inclusion in schools
Geraldine Hills
2012/pb: 978-0-415-68768-3

More Trouble with Maths: A teacher's complete guide to identifying and diagnosing mathematical difficulties
Steve Chinn
2012/pb: 978-0-415-67013-5

Dyslexia and Inclusion: Classroom Approaches for Assessment, Teaching and Learning, 2ed
Gavin Reid
2012/pb: 978-0-415-60758-2

Promoting and Delivering School-to-School Support for Special Educational Needs: A practical guide for SENCOs
Rita Cheminais
2013/pb 978-0-415-63370-3

Time to Talk: Implementing outstanding practice in speech, language and communication
Jean Gross
2013/pb: 978-0-415-63334-5

Curricula for Teaching Children and Young People with Severe or Profound and Multiple Learning Difficulties: Practical strategies for educational professionals
Peter Imray and Viv Hinchcliffe
2013/pb: 978-0-415-83847-4

Successfully Managing ADHD: A handbook for SENCOs and teachers
Fintan O'Regan
2014/pb: 978-0-415-59770-8

Brilliant Ideas for Using ICT in the Inclusive Classroom, Second edition
Sally McKeown and Angela McGlashon
2015/pb: 978-1-138-80902-4

Boosting Learning in the Primary Classroom: Occupational therapy strategies that really work with pupils
Sheilagh Blyth
2015/pb: 978-1-13-882678-6

Beating Bureaucracy in Special Educational Needs, Third edition
Jean Gross
2015/pb: 978-1-138-89171-5

Transforming Reading Skills in the Secondary School: Simple strategies for improving literacy
Pat Guy
2015/pb: 978-1-138-89272-9

Supporting Children with Speech and Language Difficulties, Second edition
Cathy Allenby, Judith Fearon Wilson, Sally Merrison and Elizabeth Morling
2015/pb: 978-1-138-85511-3

Supporting Children with Dyspraxia and Motor Co-ordination Difficulties, Second edition
Cathy Allenby, Lesley Kynman, Elizabeth Morling, Rob Grayson and Jill Wing
2015/pb: 978-1-138-85507-6

Developing Memory Skills in the Primary Classroom: A complete programme for all
Gill Davies
2015/pb: 978-1-138-89262-0

Language for Learning in the Primary School: A practical guide for supporting pupils with language and communication difficulties across the curriculum, 2ed
Sue Hayden and Emma Jordan
2015/pb: 978-1-138-89862-2

Supporting Children with Autistic Spectrum Disorders, Second edition
Elizabeth Morling and Colleen O'Connell
2016/pb: 978-1-138-85514-4

Understanding and Supporting Pupils with Moderate Learning Difficulties in the Secondary School: A practical guide
Rachael Hayes and Pippa Whittaker
2016/pb: 978-1-138-01910-2

Assessing Children with Specific Learning Difficulties: A teacher's practical guide
Gavin Reid, Gad Elbeheri and John Everatt
2016/pb: 978-0-415-67027-2

Supporting Children with Down's Syndrome, Second edition
Lisa Bentley, Ruth Dance, Elizabeth Morling, Susan Miller and Susan Wong
2016/pb: 978-1-138-91485-8

Provision Mapping and the SEND Code of Practice: Making it work in primary, secondary and special schools, Second edition
Anne Massey
2016/pb: 978-1-138-90707-2

Supporting Children with Medical Conditions, Second edition
Susan Coulter, Lesley Kynman, Elizabeth Morling, Francesca Muray, Jill Wing and Rob Grayson
2016/pb: 978-1-138-91491-9

Provision Mapping and the SEND Code of Practice

Making it work in primary, secondary and special schools

Second edition

Anne Massey

Routledge
Taylor & Francis Group

LONDON AND NEW YORK

nasen

Helping Everyone Achieve ●●●

Second edition published 2016
by Routledge
2 Park Square, Milton Park, Abingdon, Oxon OX14 4RN

and by Routledge
711 Third Avenue, New York, NY 10017

Routledge is an imprint of the Taylor & Francis Group, an informa business

First edition published by Routledge 2013

British Library Cataloguing-in-Publication Data
A catalogue record for this book is available from the British Library

Library of Congress Cataloging in Publication Data
Massey, Anne.
Provision mapping and the SEND code of practice : making it work
in primary, secondary and special schools / Anne Massey. — Second
edition.
pages cm
Includes bibliographical references.
1. Educational evaluation—Great Britain. 2. School improvement
programs—Great Britain. I. Title.
LB2822.75.M383 2016
379.1'58—dc23
2015011528

ISBN: 978-1-138-90707-2 (hbk)
ISBN: 978-1-138-90708-9 (pbk)
ISBN: 978-1-315-69518-1 (ebk)

Typeset in Sabon
by Swales & Willis Ltd, Exeter, Devon, UK

Printed and bound in Great Britain by
TJ International Ltd, Padstow, Cornwall

This book is for all the SENCOs in Kent – such a hardworking, dedicated and talented bunch

Contents

Figures

Acknowledgements

Special thanks to the following individuals who gave their time and shared their knowledge and practice so generously: Cathy Aldritt, Rowena Banks, Nigel Cates, Neil Dipple, Juliette Ede, Claire Garrett, Tina Ovenden, Ruth Palmer and Keir Williams. Your schools are lucky to have you! Thanks also to the group of deputy headteachers from the Kent Association of Special Schools (KASS) who worked with me on the changes to assessment, and in particular to Dot Gent whose wisdom and clear thinking kept me grounded.

Grateful thanks to my gorgeous daughters, my fabulous friends and those who have encouraged, inspired and influenced me, especially Diana Robinson, Julie Ely, Karen Flanagan, Peter Byatt, Jacqui Tovey, Pam Jones and Rachael Sharrad.

And finally, Kevin – your patient and marvellous support made all the difference, thank you.

Introduction

Although the world of education seems to have tipped on its axis somewhat over the last couple of years, none of the changes to curriculum, assessment or SEN that have been introduced have altered my conviction that the system of Provision Mapping is an essential part of school self-evaluation and improvement. This system has been proven to help schools ensure that the teaching of pupils with SEN and the interventions provided for any pupils who require additional and different support are fully effective. It ensures that teachers have a keen awareness of their responsibility for all pupils they teach, even when they are being taught in interventions. I ended my previous book, *Provision Mapping: Improving Outcomes in Primary Schools* with the following paragraph:

> I believe that our duty as educators requires us to ensure that all children are enjoying, participating and achieving in schools. I also believe that we have a duty to ensure that teachers are enabled to maintain an accurate view of the attainment and achievement of all pupils in their class with a minimum of bureaucracy; that they can easily identify children who need additional intervention without recourse to labelling them SEN and that those children make accelerated progress. I believe that parents want and need better, contextualised information about the provision available and should be better able to understand how to help their child at home.
>
> (p. 90)

In that book I described the system which had worked well for me during my time as a primary class teacher, school leader and SENCO. The book proved popular and it is now time for an update which will take account of the statutory changes to legislation, the new SEND Code of Practice and the adjustments to curriculum and assessment, as well as provide new guidance for secondary and special schools.

The 2015 SEND Code of Practice makes clear that the school should take a graduated approach to identifying and overcoming barriers to learning for pupils with SEN. It endorses the four stages of the cycle all schools use to track and evaluate pupil progress – *Assess*, *Plan*, *Do* and *Review* as a suitable strategy to apply when identifying, providing and evaluating support for pupils with SEN. I plan to demonstrate in this book that every school needs a system of Provision Mapping to help manage the processes in this cycle and have structured the book in such a way that it reflects its four stages. However, Provision Mapping is not just for SEN. It is a system that helps schools to successfully identify, provide and track provision for *all* pupils, irrespective of whether they have a special educational need or not. It can be used to track the impact of Pupil Premium funding on eligible pupils and can be used to drive improvement in the quality of teaching and delivery of intervention throughout the school. It can support conversation with parents and will hopefully provide them with a greater level of confidence in the ability of the school to meet the needs of their child.

Sadly, no one system of Provision Mapping fits all. Although the principles of Provision Mapping are common to all phases, the system will be structured and used differently in each. Therefore, in addition to the four chapters outlining the principles and properties of a successful Provision Mapping system, I have included three further chapters on how the Provision Mapping system should be operated in primary, secondary and special schools. As you will imagine, there is some overlap between the three systems so the reader will encounter some repetition in the three phase-specific chapters. I hope that I have given sufficient guidance in each that you need only refer to the chapter that is appropriate to your setting.

If you already have this system in place in your school you will be reassured to know that only small changes will be required to accommodate the recent changes to assessment and SEN legislation and guidance. Throughout the book you will find case studies to inform you and resources to help you implement the system and at the end of each chapter there is a checklist to help the reader identify and prioritise action in their school. I hope that you find this book easy to read and useful, and that it supports you in your efforts to improve the outcomes of the pupils in your school who require additional support whether or not they have a Special Educational Need.

Chapter 1

Provision Mapping and the SEND Code of Practice

The principles that I outlined in my previous book have been echoed in the aims of the new SEND Code of Practice: involvement of pupils and their parents, an emphasis on teacher responsibility for the progress of all pupils wherever and however they are taught, and greater aspiration for all. I was delighted that the government endorsed Provision Mapping as a way to achieve this in its revised SEND Code of Practice:

> Provision maps are an efficient way of showing all the provision that the school makes which is additional to and different from that which is offered through the school's curriculum. The use of provision maps can help SENCOs to maintain an overview of the programmes and interventions used with different groups of pupils and provide a basis for monitoring the levels of intervention.
>
> (SEND, Jan. 2015, para. 6.76)

Although, from September 2014, the government abolished the use of National Curriculum Levels, it retained league tables using end of key stage statutory assessment data. The pressure of external assessment remains but the onus is now on schools to find ways to demonstrate the in-key stage progress made by all pupils, and the impact of the provision they make on all pupils in ways that are easily understood by all stakeholders, including Ofsted. For this schools require an analysis tool that is simple and user-friendly and will enable it to provide relevant and accurate information swiftly. The Provision Mapping systems described in this book will help schools evidence the impact of their provision for the most vulnerable pupils. In addition the evaluative aspect of Provision Mapping will support schools when Ofsted inspects them.

The SEND Code of Practice that contains the guidance for implementation of the Children and Families Act 2014 was published in August 2014 and has already been updated twice since then. The Act introduced some fundamental changes to the way that SEN provision is made; how SEN is categorised, how assessments are carried out, how services should work together for the benefit of the child and how pupils and their parents should be better involved in planning and monitoring SEN provision and its funding. Because of these significant changes, schools have had to make adjustments to practice. There is a far greater emphasis on the responsibility of teachers for all of the provision a school makes for vulnerable pupils; they must ensure they can meet the needs of these pupils as well as evidence that they have done so, and to what effect. I believe that Provision Mapping can support them in all of this. Much has been written already on the changes to the SEND Code of Practice – in particular in the excellent nasen publication, *Everybody Included: The SEND Code of Practice Explained*, which sets out the changes and how they impact on children, their families and schools. I will not cover all of those changes in this book, but will describe how Provision Mapping can support schools adapt to those changes and ensure that the needs of pupils and their families are met.

Categorisation of SEN

In the consultation paper of 2011 that led to many of the changes in the new Code of Practice, the coalition government recognised that the SEN label lowers aspiration both for children and young people.

> Previous measures of school performance created perverse incentives to over-identify children as having SEN. There is compelling evidence that these labels of SEN have perpetuated a culture of low expectations and have not led to the right support being put in place.
>
> (DfE 2011b, para. 22)

If schools routinely make provision for any child who requires it, we would meet the needs of all SEN pupils by default and without having to label them such. In her book *Beating Bureaucracy in Special Educational Needs* (2008), Jean Gross cited an example of how a secondary school had removed Statements yet retained and even enhanced the provision made for its most vulnerable pupils. In its SEN review, Ofsted stressed that the effect of SEN labelling is often to lower aspiration both by and for the pupil and stated that the inconsistency in the identification of SEN does not matter if 'the total package of services and support is appropriately customised to each pupil's individual needs' (Ofsted 2010). Despite this acknowledgement the government did not (in my view) go far enough towards removing the SEN label when it made the changes it did in its new Code of Practice.

The removal of the categories of School Action and School Action Plus, and introduction of the single category SEN Support would appear to indicate that the government was trying to move away from the SEN label, but all that seems to have happened is that the number recorded as SEN has reduced. All schools have had to adjust to the new categorisation and have reviewed their SEN registers. It is my understanding that the result has often been a significant reduction in the percentage of pupils on the SEN register – just as the government intended there would be. The new category of SEN Support implies that the focus should be on support. Although the Code is not specific about what that support should be or should look like, most schools have interpreted it to mean support that is significant and substantial. This has led to schools removing those pupils from their SEN register who receive occasional, catch-up support and those who have medical diagnoses of conditions such as ADHD but receive no direct provision in school. Although the government intended to act to improve parental confidence, the change to categorisation has actually meant that many parents (who feel they have struggled long and hard to get their child's needs recognised) are now anxious that they will be overlooked once more. Schools need to find ways to reassure parents that they make the provision a child requires available, as and when they require it, irrespective of whether they have a special educational need or not.

One way that some schools have acted to ensure that parental confidence remains high is to create another register – a register for vulnerable pupils that would include all those whom staff need to be made aware of, for a range of reasons, and could include those pupils who have recently been removed from the SEN register. I think that such a register has a very important role to play in ensuring that staff awareness is raised, and may reassure some parents, but I fear that it could become just another labelling exercise. The key to maintaining parental confidence is not to label their children, but to make sure that they have confidence that the school will make available any provision that is required in a timely and effective way. Provision Maps, anonymised or personalised, and shared with parents, can provide the solution.

Despite the fact that it firmly endorses Provision Mapping, the Code of Practice seems to indicate a return to personalised plans, and although it doesn't mention them by name, it would appear that we could be heading back into the dark days of Individual Education Plans (IEPs). I think that SENCOs up and down the country had hoped that multiple IEPs, languishing in filing cabinets in SENCO offices, not used by teachers and not understood by parents, had long gone. In the new Code schools are required to agree, discuss and review Outcomes with the parents of pupils with SEN Support. It instructs schools to review these Outcomes and the provision at least three times per year. I think the principle behind such guidance is correct but fear that the interpretation of this guidance could lead schools to creating an IEP type document for every child on the SEN Register. I believe that would create a U-turn back to what we have travelled so far from in schools – the setting and reviewing of targets in a way that is dissociated from the classroom provision for the pupil. I remain of the opinion that for the majority of pupils identified as SEN Support, an anonymised class Provision Map (primary) or a personalised Provision Map (secondary) will be sufficient to identify the provision they are accessing and to be the best tool possible to demonstrate to parents that their needs are being met appropriately. In many ways this practice will normalise SEN provision for those parents – the Provision Map will contain all the intervention offered: e.g. for gifted and talented as well as SEN. If schools adopt this model they will be able to discuss Outcomes with parents in the way that the government wants, but I believe the discussion will make better sense to parents if linked to the targets for the interventions listed on the Provision Map.

Despite this, I do believe that for some SEN pupils in mainstream schools, those who have more complex needs and whom the school is funding in excess of the £6000 threshold, a more personalised plan will be required.

National funding reforms

The way that Special Educational Needs is funded in mainstream schools has changed so that it is now consistent across the country. All schools receive core funding for all pupils. In addition to this funding, all schools receive a notional SEN budget, the amount of which is determined predominantly by two factors – the level of deprivation of pupils within the school (the Income Deprivation Affecting Children Index, IDACI) and the prior attainment in English and maths of pupils on entry (for pupils currently in the school that is below 78 points for entry to Year 1 and below Level 4 for entry to Year 7). The school should use this notional SEN budget to make the provision it needs to for all its SEN pupils. The government has recognised that this budget will not be sufficient to meet the needs of pupils with more severe and complex needs in mainstream schools and so has capped the school contribution from this budget to £6000 per pupil, per year. Many pupils with SEN will cost the school far less than £6000 and their needs should be able to be met from the SEN notional budget. In schools where the notional SEN budget is insufficient to meet the demands of the SEN resourcing, the local authority (LA) will provide additional financial support.

Schools will be required to provide evidence of any spending that exceeds £6000 to the funding local authority so that it can be recompensed from the top-up funding budget the LA must make available. This will also be the pot of money from which any personal budget would be made available. Schools will therefore need to be accountable for spending and its impact if they are going to be able to access High Needs funding. Each LA will have devised its own unique mechanism for schools to claim the funding, but Provision Mapping can support a school to calculate staff cost and demonstrate impact as it will show the time a pupil spends in intervention, as well as the group size and level of qualification of the member of staff delivering the intervention.

It could be said that the introduction of this financial threshold has, in effect, re-established a category of SEN with two tiers – SEN Support costing less than £6000 and SEN Support costing more. I believe that for any pupil who is costing the school more than the nationally prescribed threshold, there should be an individual plan or Provision Plan (see Chapter 3) which details their, no doubt, multiple and varying intervention. Such a plan would go a step further than a Provision Map. It would be linked to Outcomes for the child and would provide the school with very detailed and personalised information about the interventions and their impact. Thus schools could create a clear distinction between this pupil and one whose support is far less intensive, costs the school significantly less than the nationally prescribed threshold and who could have their needs met through Provision Mapping.

There is, of course, another tier, those pupils for whom SEN Support is not sufficient and who need an Education, Health and Care Plan.

Education, Health and Care assessment

One of the principles of the new Code of Practice is that parents should tell their story as few times as possible. This was brought home to me when I heard a parent estimate that she had repeated the story of her child's SEN to different people approximately 95 times over the time her son was in education. The aim of coordinating services to jointly assess and plan to meet the needs of children and young people with SEN is commonly upheld but not always easy to achieve. Although involvement of Health and Social Care is critical to this new process, it is Education that will be the main driver of any assessment. Collaboration will ensure that information is shared widely and will hopefully reduce the number of meetings that parents have to attend, but I believe that most local authorities and the NHS will have a long way to go before shared practice is firmly embedded.

Timescales and the design and content of the documentation associated with statutory assessment have all changed, but the practice of assessment still requires schools to evidence what they have done to meet the needs of the pupil from their resources and what impact that has had. In compiling this evidence I know that schools who use Provision Mapping have found that including copies of anonymised or personalised Provision Maps or Provision Plans covering an appropriate length of time has enabled them to demonstrate action and impact without much need for additional work.

Provision and review in schools

There are numerous commercially available schemes that provide a Provision Mapping service to schools. Although I previously steered schools away from such resources, I have seen so much improvement in these over the past few years that I now believe they can provide a suitable alternative for many schools. The best of the commercial schemes provide a comprehensive Provision Mapping facility that is automatically linked to the school's database, easily accessed by staff and can usually be configured to allow direct parental access. Such schemes have a cost which some small primary and special schools may find prohibitive. I think that many secondary schools and large primary schools could benefit from such systems (as long as the system satisfies the criteria I set out in Chapters 6, 7 and 8) and many have already purchased and are using them. However, the principles and features of Provision Mapping I describe throughout this book should be common to any system whether it is a commercial web-based system or a more simple school-based system.

Provision Mapping should support schools to make links between a number of processes, to collate information, reduce paperwork and ensure that interventions are focused and effective. Although the enticement of reduced bureaucracy or the ability to evidence spending may be what prompts many schools to implement this system, I have found that its greatest value is its ability to stimulate and bring about change. It is my experience that most schools have at least one teacher who struggles to understand the needs of pupils with SEN and/or those who are underachieving in their class, and does not differentiate appropriately or make adequate provision for them. Historically, many teachers have been happy to abdicate responsibility for such pupils to the SENCO or to learning support staff and perversely, in schools where the SENCO is particularly strong, this has tended to happen even more frequently. While good leaders will be able to motivate and inspire the majority of their staff, these 'hard to shift' teachers are often the most difficult to engage in any dialogue of self-improvement and remain entrenched in a pattern of teaching that does not meet the needs of all pupils. This system has been proven to create the right conditions for such change and brings a structure and timetable that, if adhered to, ensures that change *will* take place.

Evaluated Provision Maps will enable SENCOs to identify where there is greatest need and prioritise deployment of staff. The SENCO will also be able to use the evaluation to identify where there may be staff training needs. A full analysis of the evaluation of all interventions should provide governors with information that will help them to understand the impact of the school's action better and on which they can challenge the school.

Through Provision Mapping the school can focus on the needs of *all* pupils, making no distinction between SEN and non-SEN other than to ensure that the statutory duties are complied with for all pupils with an Education, Health and Care Plan. This is therefore a system for all – not just SEN – that should address problems early and as they arise and not once they are well entrenched. It should put SEN firmly back into the classroom. It will mean that all teachers will feel more in control of what happens to pupils in their class – the pupils shouldn't disappear out to interventions that the teacher has no part in planning or evaluating. The school will be able to construct pertinent and relevant performance management targets for both teachers and support staff. Parents will better understand the support the school is providing for their child and how they can help at home. School leaders and governors will be better able to both understand and challenge the impact of the additional provision the school makes available and the school should be better placed to evidence the impact of any additional funding such as SEN top-up and Pupil Premium.

If this system is fully adopted it will lead to:

- improved class teaching and more effective intervention;
- teachers being responsible for the outcomes of all pupils in their class – not passing responsibility for SEN to anyone else;
- identification of gaps in expertise within the school and improved understanding of training needs;
- better involvement of pupils and their parents;
- SMARTer target setting;
- better self-evaluation and planning for improvement;
- better understanding of how funding is being spent and whether the school is getting value for money;
- better information for parents, governors, the LA and Ofsted;
- improved ability to reallocate resources to points of greatest need.

Chapter 2

Assess

Schools may choose to assess pupils' attainment in a variety of ways. However, it is the analysis of progress from one assessment to the next that is vital to determine whether action needs to be taken, and, where it has been taken, whether or not the action has been effective. Within Provision Mapping the purpose of data tracking and analysis is to:

- ensure that the school can understand how well pupils are achieving over the course of a year and a key stage;
- swiftly identify inadequate progress and the appropriate action to address this;
- understand how successful that action has been.

The Lamb Inquiry endorsed the Ofsted view that in schools where pupils with learning difficulties and disabilities made outstanding progress there was a 'commitment to good or better progress for all pupils' and 'teachers who challenged themselves and scrutinised data to drive improvement' (Lamb 2009, p. 22). The measurement of standards and achievement is integral to an effectively self-evaluative and successfully inclusive approach to education.

Assessment that is reliable enough to be used to track progress and demonstrate that learning has or has not taken place sits at the heart of this system of Provision Mapping. Over the past few years, schools have struggled to cope with the most significant changes to assessment in this country for some time, with the greatest impact being on the lowest attaining children. According to CASPA (Comparison and Assessment of Special Pupil Assessment)

> the government seems to have given as little consideration as usual to the specific and different assessment and accountability measures required for pupils working significantly below age-related expectations.
>
> (CASPA Newsletter, issue 13, Jan. 2015)

I do not wish to enter into the 'pros and cons' debate on the changes to assessment, but I do need to make reference to it, as sound assessment is critical when identifying whether additional provision is required, in order to be able to set SMART targets for intervention and for measuring how effective provision has been.

> In deciding whether to make special educational provision, the teacher and SENCO should consider all of the information gathered from within the school about the pupil's progress, alongside national data and expectations of progress. This should include high quality and accurate formative assessment, using effective tools and early assessment materials.
>
> (SEND, Jan. 2015, para. 6.38)

A leading adviser to the Department for Education, Tim Oates from Cambridge Assessment, explains the theoretical reasons for the changes to assessment and why the government concluded that levels should be removed in his video (www.youtube.com/watch?v=-q5vrBXFpm0). He explains that levels had become a form of 'dysfunctional labelling' in an overloaded curriculum that was being delivered with undue pace. He cites practice in Singapore and Finland as exemplary, having dramatically improved in recent years without any use of levels. He also blames a 'teaching to the test' approach and over-inflation of KS2 levels as apparent causes of the lack of confidence in assessment. However, he neglects to mention that Singapore and Finland do not use league tables; reporting progress does not impose the same pressure on schools in those countries.

In this country the 'dysfunctional labelling' and 'teaching to the test' approach has only arisen because of the government's persistent use of league tables and schools' fear of the penalties if they fail to meet floor standards: a situation that will not change as league tables are being retained.

The government stated in its principles of assessment (incidentally published long after it had proposed its reforms) that it would 'not impose a single system for ongoing assessment' but that

> schools will be expected to demonstrate (with evidence) their assessment of pupils' progress, to keep parents informed, to enable governors to make judgements about the school's effectiveness, and to inform Ofsted inspections.
>
> (DfE 2014a)

However, there *is* still a single assessment system. The new National Curriculum describes the aspects of learning that should be gained each year and describes them in relation to age-appropriate expectation. At certain points (Years 2, 6 and 11) attainment will be measured against performance descriptors and against other pupils nationally by testing; and grades or scores will be reported to parents. This system, common to all, is therefore, a single system.

Between key stages, schools may now use assessment measures of their own choosing to describe what knowledge a pupil has acquired. The expectation is that they will describe attainment in ways that link to age-appropriate learning. However, schools want to be able to measure whether pupils make progress during the academic year and many have adopted bands or sub-divisions of the age-appropriate 'level' they are working within so that they can record where progress has occurred. Each of these descriptors or 'bands' will need to be given a numerical equivalence if the data is to be entered on to an analysis system, and so we are right back where we started – pupils will be described as working within a 'band' somewhere within the curriculum they are studying and will actually attain a number of points. The only real difference is that a school-specific language of age-related expectation has replaced the common, shared language of National Curriculum Levels and schools are unsure how to categorise and measure progress.

Although those who work in special needs education were initially encouraged that the government's assessment reforms did not extend to the removal of P Scales, the removal of the continuum of assessment that the National Curriculum Levels provided renders the retention of P Scales almost pointless when tracking progress of pupils from P Levels. It means that pupils who progress beyond P Levels at some point during their education will be launched into an assessment methodology based on age-related expectations. For a pupil who achieves all of P8 in Year 3 or Year 4, is it appropriate that he/she should then progress to a curriculum that is prescribed for pupils aged 5 and in Year 1? Many schools have quickly realised that the inability to track pupils on a continuum will penalise their lowest attaining pupils. In such instances surely it would be better to be able to demonstrate progress over time in a curriculum that is meaningful and aimed at increasing opportunity for independent living and working in the future – all prioritised within the new SEND Code of Practice. At the time of writing there is no clear direction from the government on this, although it appears that the government will devise a scale as reported in their publication of the draft performance descriptors in October 2014.

> There will be some pupils who are not assessed against the P Scales (because they are working above P8 or because they do not have Special Educational Needs), but who have not yet achieved the contents of the 'below national standard' performance descriptors (in subjects with several descriptors). In such cases, pupils will be given a code (to be determined) to ensure that their attainment is captured.
>
> (DfE 2014b)

Because of these uncertainties in assessment it is even more important that schools can capture the progress made by pupils in interventions in such a way that demonstrates they have acquired a skill or construct, thus proving the success of the intervention. Schools must be able to demonstrate the impact their support achieves in ways that are clear to all and easy to understand. If this action can be incorporated into the school's progress tracking system then management and monitoring of interventions will be made easier. There are already, and will continue to be, a huge number of options when it comes to assessment systems with an ever growing number of commercial companies vying for schools' business in this area. All of them will enable a school to track pupils individually and as groups, some will meet the needs of low attainers better than others and some will have add-on features such as Provision Mapping, that make them more attractive to some schools. Each school should spend some considerable time ensuring that the system it chooses will have all of the features the school requires and will be flexible enough to adapt to any further changes to assessment. I will explain the essential features of Provision Mapping within such a system and although some of the case studies in this book make reference to certain commercial systems (and I have included examples of some), many different systems will be able to provide something similar.

Questions that will be answered in this chapter:

- What are the key principles for assessment?
- How can we use our assessment data to improve the quality of teaching?
- Which method of assessment should schools use?
- How can we be sure our assessment is reliable enough?
- When should we assess pupil achievement?
- How do we use assessment data to identify pupils in need of additional interventions?

What are the key principles for assessment?

Over the period of change to assessment during 2013 and 2014, I worked with representatives from the 24 Special Schools in the Kent Association of Special Schools (KASS), spending some considerable time reflecting on this question. Guided by the principles of assessment published by the NAHT, the KASS group shaped assessment principles that would govern practice in all of their schools, namely:

1   Assessment is at the heart of teaching and learning.
2   Analysis of assessment information will be used to improve the quality of teaching.
3   Assessment will be accurate, consistent, reliable, free from bias, understood by all and increase parental confidence.
4   Reliability of teacher assessment will be achieved and evidenced through rigorous moderation.
5   Assessment will draw on a wide range of evidence to provide a complete picture of student achievement over time.
6   Assessment will be used to set high expectations for all students, to celebrate achievement and to inform the next steps for students, their families and teachers.

These six principles are interwoven through all the main questions that will be addressed in this chapter.

Assessment can be complex and time-consuming or it can be simple and immediate – it could be a set of three-hour exams taken over several weeks or it could be as basic as thumbs up or thumbs down for understanding. All assessment should inform teaching and should be used to improve learning. There are two types of assessment: formative assessment, which can best be described as assessment *for* learning and summative assessment which can best be described as assessment *of* learning. Formative assessment informs us what we need to do to achieve the end product – the outcome measured by summative assessment. To effectively track progress and impact, schools need to make use of both types of assessment. The two have sat alongside, often over-lapping, each other in our schools for decades, but I think that Paul Black describes the difference between the two beautifully, 'When the cook tastes the soup, that's formative assessment. When the customer tastes the soup, that's summative assessment' (Black and Wiliam 1998).

In its aim to raise standards in primary and secondary schools the government has made clear its intention to continue to collect summative assessment data and use this (its analysis of end of key stage 2 and 4 statutory assessment data) to generate the measures of success (standards) against which it will hold all schools to account. Ofsted, too, has relied heavily on standardised national test data when judging the quality of a school and will continue to use this evidence to support its overall effectiveness judgment. However, in its drive to make assessment more accessible, the government has stressed the need for schools to improve their use of formative assessment and to use simple terms to describe progress so that pupils (and their parents) are better aware of what has been learned and the areas where learning still needs to be achieved.

How can we use our assessment data to improve the quality of teaching?

The new SEND Code of Practice underlines the expectation that schools will constantly strive to improve the quality of teaching. It states quite clearly that all intervention should be additional to teaching that is good or better.

> High quality teaching, differentiated for individual pupils, is the first step in responding to pupils who have or may have SEN. Additional intervention and support cannot compensate for a lack of good quality teaching.
>
> (SEND, Jan. 2015, para. 6.37)

We therefore need to ensure that teaching in our schools is sufficiently good and that it will meet the needs of the majority of pupils, with additional support required by only the very few. A fundamentally important feature of this system of Provision Mapping is that class teachers should analyse attainment data, not just to identify those pupils who require additional intervention, but primarily to improve the quality of their teaching.

Ofsted emphasises the link between good teaching and good progress in its school inspection handbook.

> Inspectors will make a judgement on the effectiveness of teaching, learning and assessment by evaluating the extent to which:
>
> • assessment information is used to plan appropriate teaching and learning strategies, including to identify pupils who are falling behind in their learning or who need additional support, enabling pupils to make good progress and achieve well.
>
> (Ofsted, June 2015, para. 149)

For teachers to be fully focused on the quality of their teaching they need to be fully aware of how much progress is being made, and by whom, at each assessment point in the year. While senior leaders will certainly need to analyse the data, we want teachers to be reflective practitioners themselves. Analysis of data is an opportunity for them to step back from the classroom and examine the key questions: how effective is my teaching, who is (and who isn't) making progress in my class and why? This is a fundamental aspect of any effective and inclusive classroom. Engaging with pupil progress data allows teachers to consider which students are fully participating and achieving in school (Booth and Ainscow 2002), and it should be they who make the first analysis of the data. Such action is of particular importance under the Teachers' Standards, in place since September 2012. The DfE expects that teachers will play a part in data analysis: 'Appropriate self-evaluation, reflection and professional development activity is critical to improving teachers' practice at all career stages' (2011c, p. 7, para. 14) and is explicit in its expectation of teachers with regard to assessment.

A teacher must:

- Make accurate and productive use of assessment
- Know and understand how to assess the relevant subject and curriculum areas, including statutory assessment requirements
- Make use of formative and summative assessment to secure pupils' progress
- Use relevant data to monitor progress, set targets, and plan subsequent lessons.

(DfE 2011c, p. 12, para. 6)

It is my experience that in schools where the data are entered by an administrator, data manager or other member of staff and the resulting analysis presented to the teachers, there is often a lack of understanding of the analysis and there can even be a lack of ownership on the part of teachers – sometimes to such an extent that they mistrust what the data appear to be showing. I believe that the act of analysing assessment and progress data is such a vital part of a teacher's duty to reflect on and improve their own practice that the requirement to collate and analyse assessment data in line with school policy should be clarified in their job description. If data analysis is not carried out effectively – either the data have been incorrectly analysed or analysis is not provided within the required timescale – the teacher should be supported through the provision of training and development opportunities and challenged through the school's appraisal and/or competency policy and procedures.

One of the key requisites for this exercise to be positive and valuable is that the system itself is manageable and easily accessible. The improvement of systems over time has been dramatic and most now enable very easy analysis, but it is no use expecting staff to carry out this task if there is limited access to the data management system. Nor can there be any hope at all that staff members will be able to carry out this task if they have not received appropriate training in how to access the system.

If, therefore, the system is set up and accessible, and teachers are entering their termly assessment data on to the school's system or on to a data analysis pro-forma we can presume that the first steps towards effective analysis of data have been achieved, and we can concentrate on *how* teachers will use the data analysis to reflect on the quality of their teaching and the quality and impact of any interventions their pupils are accessing. They should be able to use the assessment data to inform their planning, grouping and the structure of their teaching. In addition to this they should be able to understand which pupils require more personalised strategies or interventions to secure improved/accelerated progress and should use their knowledge of gaps in learning to set targets.

Senior leaders also need to be using the assessment and progress data to improve the quality of teaching. Governors should be provided with information in such a way that they can make appropriate challenge to the quality of teaching. One of the methods I have devised to achieve this is to triangulate the data from observation of teaching and learning alongside the progress being made by pupils in the class at the time of the observation and evidence from work scrutiny. Schools will probably have already devised something similar, but might like to use this resource to support their evaluation of the quality of teaching and to share evidence of that with governors, and when required to do so, their LA and Ofsted (Figure 2.1).

Which method of assessment should schools use?

Whatever method or system a school chooses to use to record, measure and evidence the progress made by its pupils between key stages, it is the accuracy of that assessment system that is of vital importance. The school will need to be able to rely on the accuracy of its assessment measures to judge progress from one point to the next and determine whether pupils are on track for the targets set for them. It will need to use this information to inform the relevant stakeholders (including parents) of the impact of its work, and under the new arrangements there will initially be significant anxiety about accuracy. It remains, however, that the key to the success of Provision Mapping is assessment that is robust and reliable.

Summative assessment is not just carried out at the end of a key stage; schools need to carry out some form of summative assessment throughout each academic year to ensure that pupils are on track to achieve targets set for them. A large number of schools have relied on the test method for in-year and in-key stage summative assessment in the past. Some have used past SATs or exam papers, whilst others have bought into one of the many different commercially available tests. Schools that use tests say they provide a sense of reliability; the tests are standardised and provide an externally validated tool with which to measure attainment and help pupils to become familiar with testing. But we must be mindful of the research that questions the validity of testing. Professor Wynne Harlen, in his presentation to the AAIA Assessment Systems for the Future conference as long ago as 2006, highlighted the problems:

- 'High stakes' testing causes frequent testing and 'teaching to the test'
- Frequent testing affects children's motivation for learning
- Teaching to the test restricts the curriculum and teaching methods
- External testing encourages more internal testing
- Reduces opportunities for formative assessment

(AAIA Conference 2006)

Teacher (anonymise for GB)	Pay scale	Previous year teaching grade	% pupils on track to make 4 points progress Subject specific	Observation 1 (date) Type, duration and subject + grade (1–4)	Observation 2 (date)	Observation 3 (date)	Observation 4 (date)	Work scrutiny comments (date)	Mentor	Additional action	Notes
Mrs Smith	UPS 3	Good	English 54%	10-10-14 PM 20 mins English 3	21-10-14 RI Follow-up 30 mins English 3			Mfl observed 10-10-14 and 21-10-14	SLT mentor appointed 22-10-14	Phonics training (booked for 15-01-15)	Main issues – pace and subject knowledge

Figure 2.1 Tracker for quality of teaching

We can thus understand how the pressures of accountability have led to such frequent testing, both external and internal, which in turn has had a negative impact on the amount of meaningful (formative) assessment carried out in schools. We can also see how the National Curriculum Levels came to be used as a tool rather than a guide and be anxious that, because the government has retained league tables, the changes to assessment since 2014 will not alter this.

Another reason to exercise caution about the use of tests as a method of summative assessment is their unreliability. The accuracy of National SATs testing has consistently been called into question since their inception. For example, research has shown that almost 30 per cent of SATS test results were inaccurate (Black *et al*. 2008). The alternative to testing as a form of summative assessment is teacher assessment which Black *et al*. indicated was the most appropriate and reliable way of measuring attainment. Mansell *et al*. stated:

> [T]eachers can sample the range of a pupil's work more fully than can any assessment instruments devised by an agency external to the school. This enhances both reliability (because it provides more evidence than is available through externally-devised assessment instruments) and validity (it provides a wider range of evidence). Together maximum validity and optimal reliability contribute to the dependability of assessments – the confidence that can be placed in them.
>
> (Mansell *et al*. 2009)

Although I agree with Black *et al*. the external pressures of accountability has meant that, just like testing, teacher assessment has not always been as reliable as it should be and as we move into an era of different assessment systems, any school selecting this as its sole method of in-year summative assessment should exercise caution. Over the past few years, the use of APP (Assessing Pupil Progress) or similar such systems has been widespread in primary, secondary and special schools. Although the pre-scribed nature of APP and its focus on moderation contributed to schools' increased confidence in the use of teacher assessment and the ability of teachers to ascribe levels accurately, this 'box-ticking' approach led to much concern over the loss of teacher professional judgment and some inaccuracy and over-levelling. Tim Oates from Cambridge Assessment decried the common and frequent use of the APP approach, as some children could be assessed to have achieved all the separate components of a level whilst still not having grasped key concepts. I agree with this and have seen it happen all too often in special schools where very small steps of progress are often tracked in such a way. Over time, a pupil can accumulate enough elements of, for example, P8 reading, that the teacher will conclude the level has been reached – however, the child may not be functioning as a P8 reader at all. I would suggest that this can be overcome by ensuring that there is a better overall understanding by teachers of the concept or learning construct and whether this has been achieved or not, as well as improved moderation. Schools should strive to achieve a balance between teacher assessment and testing and ensure that assessment of any kind should be primarily aimed at determining gaps in learning.

As long ago as 1999, the Assessment Reform Group defined assessment for learning or formative assessment as:

> [T]he process of seeking and interpreting evidence for use by learners and their teachers to decide where the learners are in their learning, where they need to go and how best to get there.
>
> (Assessment Reform Group 1999)

Good formative assessment is a constant dialogue; it should incorporate peer and self-assessment, searching questioning and elicit developmental feedback to inform the learner. In short, it should not only probe whether learning has taken place but should always be forward-looking, focused on development and making improvements in learning.

Summative assessment can be used formatively if the information it generates is used by the teacher (and the pupil) to bring about changes to practice and improve outcomes. In my previous book I was determined to minimise teacher workload and recommended the use of the summative assessment carried out in class (usually termly) to track pupil progress and measure the impact of intervention. In this edition I still suggest that summative assessment information can be used in this way, but would emphasise more strongly the importance of using any summative data formatively. Assessment evidence should increase our understanding of how pupils learn and what progress needs to be made so that we can set appropriate targets for additional intervention.

If a school wants to determine the impact of the provision it has made to meet the non-academic needs of its pupils it must employ a method suitable for measuring progress in that area. Where interventions need to be measured using an alternative assessment tool the school should plan for this within the time set aside to deliver the intervention: for instance, a baseline assessment at the start of the intervention and an opportunity to carry out a final assessment at the end of the intervention period.

Some interventions have inbuilt assessment tools and it would be sensible to use these where they are provided. But often the interventions most problematic to evidence do not have a built-in assessment tool and schools need to find the simplest and most effective tool with which to measure impact. For interventions such as social skills, nurture groups, anger management, etc. the primary aim is to improve pupils' engagement with learning. In order to achieve that, Maslow's hierarchy of needs would indicate that pupils' well-being will need to be high and that too should be tracked. Some SENCOs use tools such as the Boxall Profile for this tracking but many class teachers find it cumbersome to use and difficult to interpret. Another tool growing in popularity is the 'Scales of Well-Being and Involvement' that are part of the Experiential Education Movement. This work originated from Leuven University in Belgium under Professor Ferre Laevers.

> The basic insight within the EXE-theory is that the most economic and conclusive way to assess the quality of any educational setting (from the pre-school level to adult education) is to focus on two dimensions: the degree of 'emotional well-being' and the level of 'involvement'.
>
> (European Agency 2008)

Their programme includes simple scales against which teachers rank pupil well-being and levels of their involvement with learning through a series of observations. They are a powerful aid to teacher self-evaluation, and measurements of both well-being and involvement pre-and post-intervention would provide the necessary evidence that progress is being made in interventions that cannot be measured by progress in attainment.

Many schools still assess pupils' reading age and spelling age, but although this data can be extremely useful in some instances, I would urge caution. Many of the reading age tests test reading accuracy, whereas assessment of reading within the National Curriculum is primarily an assessment of comprehension ability and any testing means that performance is further constricted by ability in writing (the ability to record the answers). If a school chooses to engage with testing then it should select an assessment tool that measures reading comprehension age as well as reading accuracy age, and always use it alongside other formative assessment data.

Whatever method (test and/or teacher assessment) a school chooses to use to assess the progress made by its pupils should be easy to understand and meaningful to all who need to use it.

How can we be sure our assessment is reliable enough?

This is the million-dollar question. Every school will be reviewing its well-established methods of assessment in light of the changes to curriculum and assessment. However, this is not a one-off consideration; every school leadership team should pose this question regularly because if the data are not reliable, measurement of progress cannot be reliable.

Schools using tests to assess attainment should consider the issues raised earlier as well as the following:

- Does the test test what has been taught? Does it give the child an equitable opportunity to demonstrate what they have learned?
- Can we use it formatively? Will it give us the information necessary to plan for future learning?
- Have we taken steps to eliminate marker error?
- Can we detect any accuracy error? For instance, does this test give a score significantly lower or higher than that achieved by the same pupils sitting a different test or via teacher assessment?
- Is everyone using the same test?

If schools use teacher assessment they should question the validity of any data just as frequently and take steps to ensure that teacher assessment is as accurate as possible. The following questions should be regularly considered in all schools:

- Do we moderate teacher assessment often enough and well enough?
- Do we moderate with a wide range of partners?
- Do the tasks we use to assess learning measure the right aspects of learning?
- Do all teachers use the same methods for teacher assessment and do they all apply the same criteria?

There is no magic formula; there simply needs to be thorough knowledge of the concepts or constructs that need to be learned and assessed, coupled with regular moderation. Although moderation is key to ensuring assessment is reliable it is often something that schools overlook or sideline, prioritising other activities instead. This is a mistake. Moderation should be a very high priority for all schools and should be timetabled into the school's calendar at the start of the year.

It is widely accepted that moderation helps give teachers the confidence that the standards they apply in making teacher assessment judgements are accurate and consistent and that the results of those assessments are fair to pupils and of great use to schools and others in evaluating pupils' performance and progress.

Ofsted wants to ensure that school leaders engage with moderation, which secures accurate assessment:

> Inspectors should evaluate how well leaders use formative and summative assessment to ensure that pupils, teachers and parents know if pupils are achieving the expected standard or if they need to catch up. Inspectors should consider how well:
>
> - Assessment information, including test results, is used by leaders and governors to improve teaching and the curriculum
> - Leaders ensure the accuracy of assessment through internal and external standardisation and moderation
> - Schools adopt the best practice of working together to moderate assessment for year groups and the end of key stages, and come to a common understanding of attainment
>
> (Ofsted, Jan. 2015, para. 148)

One way of ensuring that all curriculum subjects are moderated regularly enough could be to prepare a moderation timetable (Figure 2.2). Moderation events should be planned once per term: in primary and special schools moderation of reading, writing and numeracy should take place in alternate terms with moderation of three other subjects (for example, science, humanities, computing) taking place in the remaining terms according to a two- or three-year cycle. In secondary schools moderation should be department specific and should take place at least three times per year but best practice would be an ongoing dialogue in departments with formal moderation with other schools built into the timetable of staff development.

All moderation activities should involve teachers and as many learning support staff as possible, particularly those who deliver literacy and numeracy interventions. They will need to be fully aware of what achievement of each literacy and numeracy construct 'looks like' if they are to support pupils effectively. One simple way of ensuring that staff and pupils know what successful learning of a construct 'looks like' is to create a display around the school of anonymised pieces of work annotated to show the specific criteria linked to each aspect – for instance a display annotated

Year	Term 1	Term 2	Term 3	Term 4	Term 5	Term 6
1	Reading	Computing	Writing	Science	Maths	Humanities
2	Computing	Reading	Humanities	Writing	Science	Maths
3	Maths	Computing	Reading	Science	Writing	Humanities

Figure 2.2 Three-year moderation timetable (primary and special)

to show appropriate use of paragraphs. This acts as a reference tool for pupils and staff alike and ensures that all are aware of what they are aiming for when aspiring to achieve the next steps.

Moderation *in* school is essential but so too is moderation with *other* schools. In particular, moderation of pupils who are working on P Scales needs to take place in a wider forum, as most mainstream primary schools and secondary schools will have limited access to examples of work at that level to enable them to make comparisons.

The other merits of inter-school moderation are that it creates opportunities for infant and junior, primary and secondary schools to moderate together, which should enable them to build confidence in each other's judgments and build trust in the information shared on transfer. In all moderation exercises, whether internal or external, the school should keep records to show the outcome of the moderation. This will be particularly useful when inspected by Ofsted as it will enable the school to demonstrate that moderation is a rigorous and thorough procedure which identifies where there are any inaccuracies. If teachers are found to be assessing inaccurately the school must take immediate action to support development in this area which should also be recorded.

In Ridge View Special School, Tonbridge, Kent, the practice around accuracy of assessment and moderation is exemplary. The school caters for mostly SLD and PMLD pupils and some very severe ASD. It is a through school, from Nursery to post-16. All pupils function well below age-related expectation.

The school rigorously adheres to a progress measure based on National Progression Guidance and assesses pupils six times per year. The heads of English and maths departments facilitate six termly workshops where teachers can raise queries over pupil assessment. Six times per year, teachers assess pupils and enter the data on to the progress tracker. The data is analysed by teachers, the leaders of English and maths and the DHT with responsibility for data. In three of the six terms, the school holds Pupil Progress Review meetings led by members of the SLT. Whenever concerns are raised about assessment at Pupil Progress Review meeting or in the workshops, a moderation panel is convened and the teacher presents assessment evidence for that pupil to a group of senior staff. This group's consideration of evidence and discussion with the class teacher ensures a more secure assessment outcome. In addition to this the school frequently engages in moderation with other similar schools and mainstream schools. Consequently, the degree of confidence in all assessment in this school is extremely high. Further to this, the school has timetabled its observations of teaching to take place in the days following Pupil Progress Review meetings so that the best links can be made between progress data and quality of teaching observed.

The use of a moderation panel is key to the success of assessment in this school as it ensures that there is rigorous and reliable assessment data upon which identification of stalled or inadequate progress can be based.

(Jacqui Tovey, Headteacher, Ridge View Special School, Tonbridge)

When should we assess pupil achievement?

This is really a question in two parts: with what frequency should assessment take place and when in the year should assessments be carried out? The frequency with which assessment should take place is often debated. Those schools in Ofsted category or falling below the government's standards are generally expected to summatively assess pupil progress six times a year. Almost all secondary schools assess pupils six times per year. Ekins and Grimes believe that three times per year is effective and recommends a pattern that allows sufficient time for learning to occur before progress is measured (2009, p. 47). If we are regularly assessing pupils formatively and have a high level of confidence in that, then the frequency of summative assessment could be less than six times per year.

The timing of assessment is worth schools considering at length. I believe that the optimum time for a first assessment is towards the end of Term 1. This is obviously the case for any school that intends to assess six times per year but for those that intend to assess less frequently (three or four times) the first assessment will still need to be early on in the year so that any fallback from the previous year may be swiftly identified and addressed. Therefore, for each pattern of assessment the first measurement should be towards the end of Term 1 and subsequent summative assessments must take place at regular intervals so that the interval over which progress is measured is broadly equal. I recommend to schools that intend carrying out assessments three times per year that they take place at the end of Term 1, half-way through Term 3 and then Term 5 (which will be aligned with SATs and external exams). However, this would mean that the pupils' end of year assessment was made prematurely, so generally I recommend a minimum of four assessments – following the pattern described above with an additional assessment made at the end of Term 6 and used to inform planning for the following year.

An example of a simplistic assessment calendar is given in Figure 2.3.

However, as term lengths vary somewhat, the main consideration should be to ensure that intervals are broadly equal and that the timing of the assessment is aligned to fit in with other related activities – for instance, parent consultation should follow soon after an assessment so that parents are being given the most up-to-date progress and attainment information.

How do we use assessment data to identify pupils in need of additional interventions?

For the purposes of discussing pupils whose progress has stalled or who are making inadequate progress, we usually make use of data for reading, writing and maths.

Model	Term 1	Term 2	Term 3	Term 4	Term 5	Term 6
Six times per year	assess	assess	assess	assess	assess	assess
Four times per year	assess		assess		assess	assess
Three times per year	assess		assess		assess	

Figure 2.3 Assessment calendar

However, assessment should be concerned with the learning taking place in all subject areas and should be used in such a way that the teacher can make links (shared with the pupil and parents) across subjects and with other data held by the school: attendance and behaviour as well as any data on well-being and social and emotional development.

It is all too easy to rely solely on attainment data when considering a pupil's progress, yet some pupils will have barriers to learning and require additional intervention in aspects other than academic development. For instance, in many secondary schools a frequently provided additional intervention is student mentoring – an intervention focused on the social and emotional aspects of learning and aimed at re-engaging pupils and enhancing their awareness of themselves as active learners. Identification of pupils in need of such an intervention will not, or should not, rely solely on their performance in English and maths. For others, progress in speech and language or physical development will be critical and measures of performance in these areas should be used to both identify a need for additional intervention and to measure its impact.

Whatever commercial system a school uses to record the progress of its pupils, it would be important to choose one that enables links to be made between these vital elements at the individual pupil level. For instance, a system that facilitates easy representation of data at an individual pupil level and represents it in a very easy to understand way, showing attendance, behaviour, attainment and progress data as well as enabling the school to demonstrate progress in other aspects such as well-being and engagement. An added advantage would be that the school can enable links for parents that allow them access to this level of data on a daily basis and the system generates reports for the school to share at more formal reporting times.

In the past there were many instances of pupils being identified for intervention by the SENCO, not by the teacher. This is still sometimes the case, particularly in secondary schools where SENCOs might use prior attainment or CATS data to identify pupils in need of additional support, when actually a subject teacher may identify others as higher priority for intervention. In my view it should be the teacher who identifies pupils in need of additional catch-up or extension interventions, and it should be teachers who constantly review the pupil's need for additional intervention. Teachers should use the summative and formative assessment information they gather to determine when progress has stalled or is inadequate, irrespective of the attainment of the pupil, and should provide appropriately effective teaching, supplemented where necessary with additional intervention away from the classroom to secure rapid and sustained improvement in progress. Some data tracking systems that RAG – denote inadequate (Red), adequate (Amber) or good (Green) – pupil progress will prompt the teacher into considering whether an intervention is required. Whatever system a school uses, it should enable such identification so that action can be taken swiftly.

Checklist for Assess

In place in our school?	Yes	No	Needs developing
Formative and summative assessment is used to measure progress.			
Assessment is reliable.			
Moderation is embedded.			
Assessment is frequent enough to allow any stalled or inadequate progress to be identified early.			
The measurement of progress is over intervals of roughly equal length.			
The timetable for assessment is appropriately aligned to activities such as parent consultation, observation of teaching and governing body meetings, and strictly adhered to.			
Teachers use their assessment data to identify the pupils in need of additional and different intervention.			

Chapter 3

Plan

Once schools have identified that there is a problem with progress or learning then they must make provision to address this. The provision a school makes to meet the needs of its pupils should not be made solely to meet the needs of SEN pupils but to meet the needs of any pupils who have stalled or inadequate progress. Whatever additional provision a school makes, it should not be made randomly or without clear rationale; it should be carefully planned with full consideration for what works and what works for the targeted pupils. It should take into consideration staff expertise, training and resources, timetable and grouping. In addition, it should be planned in such a way that all stakeholders are clear what the target for the provision is, how the effectiveness of the provision will be measured and when. The Code of Practice talks specifically of planning provision for pupils with SEN but I think that the principles it puts forward – good communication, parental engagement and joint planning – would be appropriate for all pupils in receipt of additional or different provision. In addition, it states:

> All teachers and support staff who work with the pupil should be made aware of their needs, the outcomes sought, the support provided and any teaching strategies or approaches that are required. This should be recorded on the school's information system.
>
> The support and intervention provided should be selected to meet the outcomes identified for the pupil, based on reliable evidence of effectiveness, and should be provided by staff with sufficient skills and knowledge.
>
> (SEND, Jan. 2015, paras 6.49–6.50)

In the last chapter we saw how to use assessment data to identify pupils for additional provision or support. In this chapter we will see how to set SMART targets for interventions, how effective planning can ensure that the interventions can be communicated to others, can be recorded and tracked as simply as possible by the teachers, and how evaluation of the impact of the interventions provided can be made easier for the SENCO. In this chapter I will describe a generic model of Provision Mapping that a school could use to meet the requirements to plan, deliver and review the support it provides for all its pupils, irrespective of whether they have a Special Educational Need or not. In Chapters 6, 7 and 8 I describe how the system would work best in primary, secondary and special schools respectively.

Questions that will be answered in this chapter:

- Why do schools need Provision Maps?
- What are the key elements of successful Provision Mapping?
- How do teachers set SMART targets for intervention?
- Should all interventions appear on the Provision Map?
- Should Provision Maps be costed?
- What is the SENCO's role in Provision Mapping?
- How can schools use Provision Mapping to bring about improvement in quality of interventions?

Why do schools need Provision Maps?

Ofsted's SEN and disability review in 2010 found that effective schools had:

- high aspirations for the achievement of all children and young people;
- good teaching and learning for all children and young people;
- provision based on careful analysis of need, close monitoring of each individual's progress and a shared perception of desired outcomes;
- evaluated the effectiveness of provision at all levels in helping to improve opportunities and progress;
- leaders who looked to improving general provision to meet a wider range of needs rather than always increasing additional provision.

(Ofsted 2010c, p. 31)

In order to manage the number and range of interventions that a school offers, and to be able to identify those interventions that work well and those that do not, a school needs a simple and user-friendly system. In its SEN review, Ofsted recorded examples of local authorities and schools using Provision Mapping to improve provision and outcomes for children and young people with additional needs. They defined Provision Mapping as 'an audit of how well planned interventions meet needs; it also identifies any gaps in provision':

The best Provision Mapping observed did not simply list what was available; it also showed which interventions were particularly effective. This contributed to efficient planning to meet the needs of individuals or groups, kept pupils and their parents up to date with progress following an intervention, and helped a school or a local authority to evaluate its overall effectiveness.

(Ofsted 2010c, p. 63)

If schools adopt the phase-appropriate system described in this book then all the aspects of an effective approach to meeting pupils' needs should be in place and can be sustained and improved upon. The Provision Map, if used properly, will act as a stimulus for change. It will:

- remind teachers of effective strategies to support the most vulnerable pupils;
- make links between class teaching and intervention;
- ensure that aspiration remains high for all learners, irrespective of their level of ability;
- record the progress made in interventions and the effectiveness of each, highlighting areas of strength and areas for development;
- serve as a communication aid: internally, with parents and with other agencies.

I believe firmly that it should be teachers who plan interventions for pupils – not SENCOs. We learned in the previous chapter that it is generally the teachers, those who are teaching and assessing pupils regularly, who will be best placed to identify if and when a pupil is in need of additional intervention. The teacher will also be the person best placed to set SMART targets for any intervention; from their formative assessment they should know what the gaps in learning are. Although they may need support from the SENCO, the pupil, the pupil's parents and occasionally from other agencies to devise a programme of support that will work for the child or young person, I believe that the responsibility for the intervention and its success should rest with the teacher (in every phase of education). The Code of Practice is very clear in this regard:

> The teacher and the SENCO should agree in consultation with the parent and the pupil the adjustments, interventions and support to be put in place, as well as the expected impact on progress, development or behaviour, along with a clear date for review.
>
> (SEND, Jan. 2015, para. 6.48)

The involvement of pupils and their parents will be critical and should be prioritised in every school. The SEND Code of Practice guidance is that schools should meet with parents of pupils with SEN at least three times per year to discuss their outcomes and review intervention. The vast majority of parents will want to engage fully with the school in the setting and evaluating of targets, but not all will. Where parental engagement is low or non-existent, schools should continue to plan for, and deliver, intervention for any pupil. I believe that Provision Maps can support and enhance parental engagement and I know that many parents feel better informed of their child's provision by a Provision Map, which sets the provision in context of that provided for the whole class or year group, than they have done in the past by an IEP.

What are the key elements of successful Provision Mapping?

Teachers are all extremely busy people and will need an easy to use system to help them monitor the additional interventions their pupils are accessing. I demonstrate in later chapters of this book systems that work well in primary, secondary and special schools, with relevant adaptations to suit different organisational models and phase-specific guidance on involving pupils and their parents. I acknowledge that there will be differences between primary and secondary schools in the planning and monitoring of interventions and special schools will need yet another model – sadly there is no one model that will fit all – but in this chapter I will attempt to outline the elements that are key to the success of a Provision Mapping system in any phase.

The use of Provision Maps as described in this book has evolved from earlier models (Gross and White 2003; Ekins and Grimes 2009; Massey 2013). Although, strictly speaking, the Provision Map is nothing more than a management tool, it should be more than just a list of interventions in place. It can be evaluative and can link several school processes together. It should be used to aid planning and prioritisation of resources and can also help staff to monitor the amount of time pupils spend away from the classroom accessing intervention programmes. Collated and evaluated Provision Maps can provide evidence on the impact of interventions for the school's self-evaluation and anonymised class Provision Maps (primary) or personalised Provision Maps (secondary and special) can be shared with parents so that they better understand the provision being made for their child and the ways they can help at home.

In all phases or types of school, Provision Maps should be held on a central and accessible system and kept to a simple format as they need to be easily understood by all those who need to use them: teachers, support staff, supply teachers, other agencies, senior leadership teams and parents. Schools may choose to present them in a different format or add additional information, but the key elements of a Provision Map should be the same for any school:

- Each Provision Map should be clearly dated so that the period of intervention is measurable.
- There should be a record of, or a link to, guidance on effective quality teaching strategies (Wave 1) that would apply to the group for whom the Provision Map is written.
- Details of targeted or personalised support, to include:

  o   name of pupil
  o   title of intervention
  o   length, duration and frequency of sessions
  o   qualification level of the person delivering intervention (i.e. TA or Teacher)
  o   entry data (if appropriate)
  o   SMART target or outcome
  o   exit data (if appropriate)
  o   impact.

The Provision Map should be a working document. I believe that teachers will naturally be anxious that pupil absence from their classroom means that pupils are away from their good teaching. If pupils are to leave the classroom to access additional intervention, teachers will want to track that the intervention is having sufficient impact to merit that absence. As such, the Provision Map should be an integral part of any teacher's planning and monitoring activity and should be regularly considered and updated if necessary.

I am more and more convinced of the potential benefit to schools of using commercial systems that produce Provision Maps linked to the school's data on attendance, behaviour and academic progress; but not if the Provision Map it produces is simply a list of interventions delivered and has no facility to evaluate the impact of each intervention. If the school is to use a commercial system then it should ensure that the system enables the:

- entry of intervention groups;
- identification of the person responsible for the intervention (the teacher);
- identification of the person delivering the intervention (usually the TA);
- entry of intervention target(s);
- entry of appropriate data (e.g. Reading Age);
- assessment of the outcome of the intervention target on the Map;
- automatic generation of a personalised list of interventions and their impact on an individual that can be shared with parents;
- analysis of the impact of all interventions across the school.

These aspects will be explored further in the phase-specific chapters on Provision Mapping, but are the key elements that a school should demand of any purchased system.

How do teachers set **SMART** targets for additional intervention?

Despite the fact that the target-setting acronym SMART has been around for a long time, I am often invited by schools to deliver training for staff on how to write SMART targets for interventions. The targets for intervention should largely be determined in collaboration with pupils and their parents and should draw on information from the formative assessment information – or from summative information used formatively.

If we are clear at the outset about the purpose of the intervention and what will be achieved in the time allocated, we should be able to measure whether that has been achieved or not. The key to success of Provision Mapping in any phase or stage of education is the quality of target setting. I think this is where many teachers fail to use Provision Mapping correctly and it is one of the reasons it has sometimes been seen as a chore rather than an integral part of planning for learning. Once teachers realise that it is their responsibility to both identify pupils in need of additional intervention as well as plan the intervention and monitor its impact, they will see the importance of target setting. It is not sufficient to set targets such as – 'will make progress in reading' (even if that is quantified – 'will make two points progress in reading'). The target for the intervention should be linked to the formative assessment and should detail the specific aspects to be addressed. If teachers are in doubt about what an intervention target looks like, I suggest that they consider how they would explain the target to parents in such a way that they could describe how parents could help at home. Thus, 'will make 2 points progress in reading'

could become

'will be able to recognise and use punctuation (full stops and commas) appropriately when reading, so that reading pace and comprehension is increased by the end of the intervention (6 weeks)'.

This is a **SMART** target –

- **Specific** (taken from gap analysis of assessment information),
- **Measurable** (can the pupil now recognise full stops and commas when reading?),
- **Achievable** (assessment information tells us this is the next step),
- **Relevant** (is being reinforced in the classroom) and
- **Timed** (will be achieved by the end of the stated intervention period).

Teachers need to share the targets with both pupils and their parents; only SMART targets like this will make any sense to either. The target should describe an achievable small step that will be accomplished within the timeframe set and should be something that is related to current learning. It should not concentrate on a skill or area of knowledge that will not be reinforced in the classroom and could not be supported additionally by parents at home. For instance, a target linked to shape would not be appropriate if the class were currently learning about measuring time. It should be specific enough that all are aware of the aspects to be covered and the outcome can be measured; for instance, 'to be able to accurately read and understand the notation of the 24hr clock and read a bus timetable' would be more specific and measureable than 'be able to tell the time'.

Within the cycle of Assess, Plan, Do and Review many of the phases merge into one another. For instance, the views of parents and pupils will be gathered during the Review phase and will inform and guide target setting for the future – the next Planning phase. Their views and knowledge of 'what works' for this pupil will be vital in ensuring success but in many instances pupils and parents will expect teachers to guide them in the target-setting process and will understandably expect that teachers will be best placed, through use of their assessment knowledge, to identify the gaps in learning that need to be addressed.

When the school wants to evaluate the impact of all its interventions, it should really be against the targets, not against an arbitrary measure of points or levels of progress. The previous example of a SMART target would illustrate how it is sometimes unreasonable to expect that, over a short period of time such as a few weeks or a few sessions, pupils accessing interventions will make progress that could be measured by a test. In this instance the pupil may well be reading with better pace and their understanding of the text will no doubt be improved following the intervention, but it would not necessarily be evidenced through a test score. However, if the target has been sufficiently SMART it will be possible to easily measure whether the intervention has been successful or not.

What schools really want to know is whether the intervention has been delivered in such a way that it has been effective, because the real purpose of evaluation of intervention is to determine whether it is worth doing again with pupils; either the same group or a different one. When evaluating the impact of all the interventions and whether they should be continued or discontinued, the SENCO will want to consider the number or proportion of pupils who have met the targets set for them and this will be discussed further in Chapter 5. There is obviously one caveat to this method of evaluation – the targets must have been suitably challenging. I would prefer to add 'aspirational' to the 'achievable' in the SMART acronym. It will be of vital importance that the person monitoring the additional interventions across the school (usually the SENCO) is aware of the need for aspiration and is satisfied that all targets set are just that. We know from research that successful intervention can result in accelerated progress and we should be aspirational enough to expect that from the intervention we provide.

Should all interventions appear on the Provision Map?

There is such a risk of duplication of paperwork when it comes to additional intervention that schools must exercise caution. The school will be making provision to meet the needs of disadvantaged pupils as well as those who have SEN and/or need to catch up. The Provision Map can, and should, be used to capture all the interventions that are funded through Pupil Premium. This could be easily achieved by identifying individual pupils on the Provision Map; a different colour font or an asterisk to identify them would do so without breaching confidentiality. Web-based systems that are linked to schools' management information systems usually automatically identify these pupils on the Provision Maps. When we look at how to review the impact of intervention in Chapter 5 we shall see how an overview of the impact of all interventions is achievable, including that funded through Pupil Premium. We shall also see how to use a simple analysis tool to show the impact of this funding and how the school is narrowing the gap in achievement between those with the funding and those without.

For those pupils receiving support as part of an EHC Plan it is best to clarify what should be recorded and where. Where an EHC Plan is in existence, there should be very clear guidance in Section F around the provision to be made for the pupil:

> [I]t must be detailed and specific and should normally be quantified, for example, in terms of the type, hours and frequency of support and level of expertise.
>
> (SEND, Jan. 2015, para. 9.69)

The provision for this individual does not need to be included on the Class Provision Map if an individualised plan such as one shown in Figure 3.1 is used. All the intervention and its impact can be tracked here. However, if the pupil is included in a group intervention then his/her name should appear on the Provision Map in that group so that a correct analysis of the impact of the intervention over the whole group can be calculated. Whilst it is helpful for primary staff to see and track very personalised intervention such as speech and language therapy or counselling on the Class Provision Map this could lead to duplication which staff would find justifiably frustrating. However, teachers should be aware of the intervention that a pupil is receiving from outside agencies and the targets set for those interventions so that they

Provision Plan	Name:				Date:
The Outcome I am working towards					
Changes that will be made to the National Curriculum or my course					
What I need to help me	*Resources/training for which funding has been applied/agreed*				
Ways to help me					
Extra support (intervention) I need	How often I need this and who will provide it	What I need to achieve this term	How well did it work?	Date	

In-year Review

1	Young person/parent/carer signature	Provider signature	Date
2	Young person/parent/carer signature	Provider signature	Date
3	Young person/parent/carer signature	Provider signature	Date

Figure 3.1 Provision Plan

can be supported and reinforced in the classroom. If this is best achieved by recording the provision on the Provision Map, even if it means duplication, then that should be what happens.

In special schools, Provision Mapping might be seen as just another paper exercise, as all pupils will have an EHC Plan and therefore will have their provision clearly described. However, provision will, and should, be adjusted over the course of a school year and teachers in special schools need to manage this change just as teachers in mainstream schools do. In chapter 8 I describe how Provision Mapping in special schools can help teachers to manage the provision and maintain a clear and up-to-date overview of the impact of the intervention being delivered.

Should Provision Maps be costed?

Since the publication of my first book with its proposals for a Provision Map, national funding arrangements for SEN have changed. The model I suggested then did not include the costing of provision as I felt anxious that such an action could lead to cessation of an intervention (because of expense) irrespective of its effectiveness. Since the changes to SEN funding, schools will need to be able to demonstrate that they have met the nationally prescribed threshold (currently £6000) for spending on a pupil with SEN if they want to access additional 'top-up' funding from the local authority. As well as needing to evidence this funding, schools also need to evidence Pupil Premium funding. Despite this, I remain sure that the costing of interventions should not appear to teachers or parents on a Provision Map. By showing clearly the timing and staffing arrangements on a Provision Map parental confidence will be raised and it will be able to calculate cost of intervention if necessary.

Commercial Provision Mapping systems mostly have the facility to cost interventions built in and many make useful links to Pupil Premium spending – identifying when an intervention is funded through that stream. The commercial systems make the costing of interventions easier to achieve than a school-based system would, but I think this facility should be hidden and only available to an individual with administrator rights.

The mechanism for schools to demonstrate spending and access top-up funding will differ from authority to authority, but the need for schools to be able to demonstrate spending, and its impact, will be common to all. When a pupil in a mainstream school is eligible for high-needs funding (whether they have an EHCP or not) their needs will no doubt be substantial and complex and I believe that at this point a class or department Provision Map will not be sufficient to record and track their many and varied interventions. Any system would need to be able to generate a list of the interventions provided for an individual, their impact and the total cost over the course of the year.

Schools that have purchased an electronic Provision Mapping system should check that their system allows them to calculate spending on one pupil over one year with the ability to vary the start and end date to fit in with Annual Review. For schools that have not purchased a commercial system that produces an individual's costed Provision Map but are using their own system, I would recommend that they record all the intervention to address such high level needs on one document, the Provision Plan (Figure 3.1). This document should make clear the links to the outcomes sought for the pupil over the next phase or stage of his/her education. This Provision Plan has been designed to be similar to the Provision Map in style and therefore provide a degree of consistency for staff and parents who are used to Provision Maps. For any pupil in receipt of High Needs funding, the school will need to make an annual review of funding, action and impact and this document can be used for those purposes.

What is the SENCO's role in Provision Mapping?

The SENCO's role in Provision Mapping is to:

- provide advice on interventions and strategies;
- ensure that intervention targets are SMART and sufficiently aspirational;
- evaluate the impact of interventions across the school;
- ensure that any training needs are met;
- ensure resources are adequate;
- discuss and agree prioritisation of provision with the SLT;
- ensure this information is shared with relevant bodies – governors, parents, LA, other schools, etc.

In this system it is the teacher who should be responsible both for the determination of the provision and the evaluation of it; the role of the SENCO is to advise on the most appropriate intervention and to support the teacher's evaluation by contributing additional evidence gathered from observations of the delivery of interventions. It is also the SENCO's responsibility to collate all the class Provision Maps following a Pupil Progress Review period and to evaluate and record the impact of the interventions across the school to inform the school's self-evaluation and the governors (see Chapter 5). Any intervention that is proving to be less effective than it should, is less effective than it has been in the past or is less effective in one class than in another should be investigated by the SENCO and action taken. Where intervention is new or where improvement is necessary, the SENCO should identify appropriate training and ensure that the relevant staff members access this and that impact is positive.

Although it may be the class teacher who selects an intervention, support with resourcing may be requested of the SENCO. It is usually the SENCO who has access to the school's SEN budget and who can purchase additional resources. Through links with other schools, the SENCO may be able to source or borrow resources such as assessment materials, augmentation aids, etc.

A key action following Pupil Progress Review meetings should be a discussion between the SENCO and the other members of the SLT to ensure that the team has accurately identified priorities for further development (for instance, that school-wide training on ASD needs to be provided) and is aware of their responsibility, both collectively and individually, in supporting the school to achieve those priorities.

It is definitely *not* the SENCO's role to write the Provision Map for teachers, and schools should beware of falling into this trap. In many schools, efficient and conscientious SENCOs have completed Provision Maps for teachers in the misguided belief that it is the completion of the Provision Map that is of paramount importance – it is not. The most important feature of this system is that it encourages the teacher to assume greater responsibility and accountability for the progress of all pupils in the class, irrespective of any SEN. A perfectly completed Provision Map done *for* them and not *by* them will be counter-productive and will only reinforce their view that pupils who do not make adequate progress are 'someone else's problem'.

It is also not the SENCO's job to send out Provision Maps to parents. The Provision Map is an excellent way of communicating with parents and should be shared with them, but it is usually teachers who should do this, not SENCOs (see Chapter 5), and it should be information that is shared and discussed during a face-to-face meeting.

In my experience, one of the benefits of adopting this Provision Mapping system is that, through greater accountability, teachers become more responsible for the outcomes of all pupils in their class. As they become more involved with monitoring and evaluating the impact of interventions and assume responsibility for the target setting of interventions as well as in the classroom, the number of interventions they identify as necessary to secure good progress usually reduces. Generally, those teachers who have historically asked for a large number of interventions to support pupil progress in their class come to realise the importance of reducing the frequency and time a child spends accessing interventions that are not having sufficient impact upon progress. Where this does not happen SENCOs should play a part in challenging the number of interventions in place. Where there are a large number of interventions proposed by a teacher, the SENCO might work with the teacher to consider the order of priority of the interventions and the impact needed. There should be clear reasons given as to why an intervention is necessary and the teacher should be prepared to enter into a 'must, should, could' conversation:

- which interventions **must** happen;
- which **should** happen;
- which, in an ideal world, **could** happen.

In special schools the monitoring of Provision Maps should be the responsibility of one member of the SLT. This will be explored further in Chapter 8.

How can schools use Provision Maps to bring about improvement in quality of interventions?

Through his research, Greg Brooks (2013) has established that effective intervention can bring about double the rates of expected progress in literacy. If the school is expecting such accelerated progress from its interventions then I believe it is appropriate to link the intervention targets to the performance management process for the teaching assistants who deliver them. As part of the performance management process the school should be making relevant training available and should be providing the staff with any support required to help achieve the targets set. This, in turn, should improve the quality of delivery of the interventions and ultimately their effectiveness.

It is important here to consider how TAs are deployed in this system. In most primary schools, support staff, the majority of whom are attached to classes, deliver interventions. Many schools report that their teachers want a class-based TA working alongside them in the classroom but there is no evidence to support the impact of such practice upon pupil progress (Blatchford *et al.* 2009; Higgins *et al.* 2011), and Ofsted reported 'High-quality intervention from members of the wider workforce who had qualifications and training that were directly relevant to the specific areas in which they were working had the greatest impact on learning' (Ofsted 2010c, p. 5). All classes will have different needs, and it is unlikely that all support staff would have the skills necessary to deliver such a wide range of interventions. It would be more logical to have a highly trained team of specialist staff that can provide support across the school in specific areas of additional intervention. For instance, a member of the support staff who has accessed an intensive training course in speech and language would be best deployed to deliver speech and language programmes across the school instead of delivering a wide range of non-specific interventions (for which no training has been accessed) in only one class. Another member of the support staff may have far greater experience with and the skills necessary to deliver numeracy interventions; yet another may be very effective in leading social skills intervention. It would appear short-sighted to limit such staff to delivering interventions in one class or year group and more effective to ensure that they are deployed more widely across the school in their areas of specialism. To reinforce the importance of this practice I suggest that schools change the title for TAs or LSAs (Learning Support Assistants) and make reference to their enhanced training and expertise by calling them support specialists. Where I have observed this practice in schools there has been a very positive impact and many support staff have reported feeling more valued and respected by pupils and their parents.

The use of specialist support staff is more common in secondary schools and, as will be explained more fully in the chapter on secondary Provision Mapping, I encourage secondary schools to 'attach' some support staff to English and maths departments where they can be specifically trained to deliver interventions that link closely to current teaching (see Chapter 7).

It would be prudent of any school to audit the skills of the teaching and support team on a regular basis and to determine where there are gaps in expertise so that training and development may be appropriately delivered. Such an audit will be informed by the evaluation of the impact of intervention, particularly where a number of similar interventions are being delivered by a number of different staff across the school, and also by observations of delivery of interventions carried out by members of the SLT or the SENCO. It is my experience that the majority of support staff members welcome the opportunity to make links between the aspirational targets for the interventions they are delivering and quantifiable performance management pupil progress targets, against which their performance may be measured. Should a SENCO wish to audit the practice of teaching staff this tool could support that process (Figure 3.2).

Name: _____   Class: _____

Standard	No experience/ information	Basic knowledge/ awareness	Confident	Very confident
How to create a warm, safe and empathetic ethos to support children's emotional well-being.				
Basic awareness of how to incorporate high incidence SEN within the classroom, e.g visual timetables, differentiation, personalised activities.				
The ability to take account of individual children's learning styles and adjust teaching accordingly.				
How to inspire parental confidence by establishing a reciprocal relationship with them as partners in their children's learning and development through good exchange of information and by using resources flexibly to meet needs.				
The ability to respond to unpredicted need by flexible use of the environment, e.g. time out space.				
Following a care plan for pupils who require one to maintain their health.				
Using ICT to overcome barriers to learning.				
Able to implement short term interventions to secure improved progress for children and young people.				
Using provision mapping to assess and record interventions and pupils progress.				
Assessing the impact of interventions.				
Differentiating classroom activities to enable SEN children to access the same learning as the main group in the class.				
Aware of the key requirements of the SEN Code of Practice.				
Aware of the CAF process.				
Aware of Equality Legislation.				
Aware of Ofsted expectations for learners with SEN.				

Figure 3.2 Minimum standards for all learners: teacher audit

© 2016 *Provision Mapping and the SEND Code of Practice*, Anne Massey, Routledge

(continued)

Standard	No experience/ information	Basic knowledge/ awareness	Confident	Very confident
Promoting a positive regard for individual difference in the way that they learn and socialise including children with learning difficulties and/or disability.				
Careful consideration of the requirements of homework activities.				
Using alternative recording methods.				
Planning and providing differentiated activities.				
Focus on key concept/objective in the lesson.				
Peer support and sensitive grouping/pairing for practical activities.				
Providing spellings of all new subject specific words.				
Learning environment and lesson structure that incorporates visual, auditory and kinaesthetic elements, providing for smaller group and individual teaching.				
Adapted general classroom equipment – scissors, pencil grips.				
Word banks, number lines, subject and topic specific words.				
Visual timetable, 'Active Listening' cues, labeled environment at appropriate visual recognition level.				
Multi-sensory approaches, e.g. visual prompts.				
Alternatives to writing.				
Use simplified language to explain concepts.				
Ensure all children are challenged to respond by asking open ended questions.				
Positive role models of learning disability used within the curriculum.				

Standard	No experience/ information	Basic knowledge/ awareness	Confident	Very confident
Ensuring that children and young people have an awareness of a range of strategies for effective communication.				
To reduce barriers to learning for children and young people with communication and interaction needs through the provision of an appropriate learning environment: • calm area/ haven • differentiated visual support • effective use of resources • work stations.				
Able to identify the information carrying words that are important for communicating key concepts.				
Pupil centred planning to ensure optimum engagement in learning through developing and supporting social and independence skills.				
Regular monitoring of involvement and engagement, e.g. use of Leuven scales.				
A range of additional activities – e.g. circle time, social skills, buddies, talk partners, etc.				
'Time-out' facility – short term measure with the aim of returning to class.				
Promote opportunities for the development of social interaction skills throughout the school day.				
Use of positive language to promote self esteem.				
Use of tone of voice to deescalate situations.				
Awareness of subliminal messages conveyed through body language and posture.				
Use of quality listening to manage interaction and engagement.				

Checklist for Plan

In place in our school?	Yes	No	Needs developing
A system that enables us to evaluate the impact of the interventions.			
Pupils and their parents are involved in the planning.			
Assessment information is used to set SMART targets.			
Interventions are prioritised and the number of interventions proposed is reducing over time.			
Interventions are delivered effectively and targets are used to support staff appraisal target-setting processes.			
There is a clear understanding of the role each member of staff has in the Provision Mapping process.			

Chapter 4

Do

The SEND Code of Practice makes clear the teachers' responsibility for the management of additional provision:

> The class or subject teacher should remain responsible for working with the child on a daily basis. Where the interventions involve group or one-to-one teaching away from the main class or subject teacher, they should still retain responsibility for the pupil. They should work closely with any teaching assistants or specialist staff involved, to plan and assess the impact of support and interventions and how they can be linked to classroom teaching. The SENCO should support the class or subject teacher in the further assessment of the child's particular strengths and weaknesses, in problem solving and advising on the effective implementation of support.
>
> (SEND, Jan. 2015, para. 6.52)

In the busy life of a school, the ease of use of a system to support teachers' management of interventions will be key to their overall success. Published research on the effectiveness of interventions invariably notes that any intervention programme delivered according to the prescribed methodology, with the correct frequency and by trained staff, will usually have a positive impact. In this chapter we shall see how Provision Maps can help schools to manage interventions and how they can be used as part of target-setting conversations with pupils and for staff appraisal. But Provision Mapping is not just concerned with delivery and monitoring of interventions: it should also support teachers to meet the needs of all pupils they teach through the use of highly effective teaching strategies.

Questions that will be answered in this chapter:

- Can the Provision Map help to track pupil absence from lessons?
- Can Provision Maps help improve the quality of teaching?
- How can schools be sure that any improvement is sustained?
- Do Provision Maps help teachers to track interventions and share targets with pupils?
- Do Provision Maps help us to find out what works?

Can the Provision Map be used to track pupil absence from lessons?

There is a very critical balance to be achieved between the amount of time a pupil spends in intervention and the amount of time he/she spends accessing high quality teaching within the classroom. In the majority of primary schools interventions are usually delivered to avoid removing the pupil from literacy or numeracy sessions and in secondary schools there is a general aim to avoid any absence from core subjects and exam subject lessons. This leaves a finite time for intervention and causes problems when trying to timetable staff to deliver the interventions. Some mainstream schools have introduced pre- or post-school interventions. Whilst very effective in many cases, such arrangements have their own barriers to success – getting pupils to arrive in school on time to access pre-school interventions and/or sustaining pupils' energy and enthusiasm for learning at the end of the day, along with transport difficulties for those living some distance from the school, mean that many of the interventions are best delivered during the school day. In any Provision Map there should be a way to enable teachers to record the time and frequency of any intervention so the time spent away from the classroom could be quickly established. I believe that if this type of scenario occurs – 'if he is not able to make progress in my class he must need lots of additional intervention' is symptomatic of an abdication of teacher responsibility for SEN. This is so wrong; it will always be the quality of classroom teaching that makes the biggest difference to pupil progress – not the number of interventions they access. Teachers must always reflect on the total length of time their pupils are absent from lessons and ensure that any absence from the classroom is absolutely essential.

In secondary schools electronic registration systems should pick up when a pupil is missing too many lessons, but may not register when only part of a lesson is missed. If a school uses a commercial system with a Provision Mapping facility it should check that the system has the facility to record the timing and frequency of the interventions that would enable a calculation of time spent accessing interventions to be made.

Can Provision Maps help improve the quality of teaching?

The explicit message in Ofsted's 2010 SEN review was that good teaching in the classroom makes the biggest difference to pupil outcomes. All pupils have a right to experience good or better teaching but there is always room for improvement, and schools have a responsibility to ensure that teachers have the necessary skills and knowledge to meet the needs of all pupils, but particularly those pupils who are vulnerable to experiencing barriers to participation and engagement with learning. No matter how effective additional interventions are, they will not make up for teaching that is less than good. In Chapter 3 I shared the essential elements of a Provision Map, one of which is the listing of strategies (low or no cost actions that will enhance quality of teaching) on the Provision Map, or on a database in some way linked to it. This element of the Provision Map system is often overlooked or little used, when in fact I believe it to be the most useful element of all in improving quality of teaching. There are materials available online to support teacher awareness of appropriate classroom strategies for the most frequently encountered need types – such as the Advanced Training Materials for autism; dyslexia; speech, language and communication; social, emotional and behavioural difficulties; moderate learning difficulties (www.advanced-training.org.uk) and the IDP materials now hosted by nasen at www.idponline.org.uk. These materials should be used with staff both to raise general awareness and to support specific members of staff whose teaching is not as inclusive as it should be.

It is important to mention here the critical aspects of good classroom teaching:

- sound understanding of the levels pupils are working at and next steps for development;
- good differentiation;
- good understanding of strategies that would successfully support pupils who are vulnerable to underachievement and those strategies needed to support the high-frequency need types (ASD, ADHD, dyslexia, speech and language, etc.);
- planned and effective use of additional staff, ICT and resources;
- lessons that are challenging and well paced with frequent checks of understanding.

How to achieve consistently good or better teaching across the school will be the single most important issue facing any school's SLT, but the solution to some issues may well be already within the school. Many staff will have a wealth of experience and have developed a range of effective strategies over the years, while others will have new ideas they have recently tried out or ideas picked up from training, and the sharing of 'what works' will be critically important.

Good teachers can find it difficult to 'blow their own trumpets'; they often prefer to share what hasn't worked rather than what has, and schools seldom structure opportunities for sharing good practice into their plan for CPD. I suggest schools timetable opportunities for sharing good practice into the annual calendar (professional development meetings) and ensure that all members of staff contribute to this activity. I suggest that in secondary schools staff are regularly reminded of, and invited to contribute to, the advice and resources to meet the needs of pupils within the classroom and that this is made available on the school's system. In primary schools I suggest that time be set aside at a staff meeting at least three times per year when the quality teaching box on the Provision Map can be updated. Use of this aspect of Provision Mapping will be explored further in Chapters 6–8 on phase-specific Provision Maps.

In addition to the sharing of good practice within departments and across the school there should be an annual review of staff awareness of SEN-associated teaching strategies and an audit of training needs. All schools should be evaluating the impact of training on the performance of their staff and should be able to share this information with governors. As schools find it increasingly difficult to release staff to attend training, from both a cover and a cost point of view, it becomes increasingly more important to get 'value for money' from all training. Schools should have an established practice of evaluation and dissemination or feedback to other staff following each attendance at training, and should be able to evidence the impact of training on teaching and outcomes.

How can schools be sure that any improvement is sustained?

Through the regular and frequent review of pupil progress, triangulation of this information with teaching observations and work scrutiny, as well as scrutiny of impact of interventions, a school can guarantee that a focus on the quality of teaching is sustained. If this system is linked into the appraisal cycle the focus will be ongoing and developmental.

Whatever action is identified to address performance should be linked to the school's appraisal process. It would be sensible for schools to align the appraisal cycle with the Pupil Progress Review cycle to ensure that the progress targets are set and reviewed in relation to the most recent and relevant pupil progress data. It would therefore be appropriate to arrange the target-setting meetings for a week or so after the first stage in the assessment and review cycle usually at the end of Term 1. The appraisal of support staff should also be aligned to this cycle as the setting of measurable intervention targets should enable the pupil progress targets for support staff to be clearly defined. In addition to the pupil progress targets, professional development targets can also be linked to Pupil Progress Review. Where whole-school or individual training needs are identified as a result of data analysis and Pupil Progress Review, targets should be set and training accessed to ensure a successful outcome.

Do Provision Maps help teachers to track interventions and share targets with pupils?

Once the Provision Map has been agreed and staff identified to deliver each intervention, there should be an opportunity created in the timetable to ensure that the staff who will be delivering the interventions are adequately prepared for them. The targets for each intervention need to be fully understood and any resources prepared. Time will need to be allocated in order to achieve this. Schools seem to be reluctant to take a break from the delivery of interventions even for a short period of time – the world will not end if there is no reading intervention for one or two days a term. I suggest that, following the drafting of the Provision Map, interventions (other than those that are part of a Statement or EHC Plan) are suspended for a few days. This will allow support staff to prepare themselves and any equipment or resources necessary; to carry out any baseline assessment (though this should be minimal); and to familiarise themselves with the intervention targets as well as pupils who may be new to them or to the intervention.

One of the keys to positive outcomes for intervention is effective communication between the person delivering the intervention and the teacher responsible for it.

In a model where specialist TAs or departmental TAs deliver interventions across a school this can be problematic. Many TAs work part-time and often have additional duties at lunch and break times so it can be hard to find time to talk with the teacher. A simple solution is to develop a system for recording any relevant information and ensuring that the teacher responsible for the intervention is quickly alerted to any issues identified by the TA. I recommend a basic pro-forma to record the pupils accessing the intervention, their attendance, the targets and any observations by the TA of issues relating to behaviour or progress that the teacher needs to be made aware of.

In the period following the Pupil Progress Review meetings, when the majority of interventions are temporarily suspended, the TA can transfer the targets for the intervention from the Provision Map to the intervention record sheet and at this point an opportunity will be created for a planning dialogue about the targets between the TA and the class teacher (Figure 4.1). The linking of these targets to the TAs' appraisal targets will reinforce their importance and the teacher can be confident that the intervention will be appropriately focused.

Class 4			Date: Term 4					Teacher: Mrs FD TA: Mrs C			
Intervention: Writing			**Timing, frequency and duration: 3x 30 x 4**								
Pupils: Amy, Joe, Dan, Fred, Bob, Max											
Date	10/4	12/4	13/4	18/4	20/4	21/4	25/4	27/4	28/4	5/5	7/5
Absence	Amy	X illness		Joe	Joe			X INSET	Dan Bob		
Targets			**Observation and progress notes**								
To be able to write in complete sentences.			12/4 Joe very disruptive – lacks confidence								
			13/4 Joe made some effort but easily distracted								
To be able to use marking ladders to self check punctuation successfully.			20/4 Joe's absence has meant the group has made more progress over this 2 weeks								
			21/4 Dan making good progress, self checking well								
			28/4 Dan and Bob in swimming gala, Joe very disruptive to the girls today								

Figure 4.1 Intervention record sheet completed

The intervention record sheet should be used as a regular communication tool. It is important to keep such systems of communication simple and the best practice I have observed has been just that: in one primary school all the intervention record sheets for each class are kept within a folder or file in the classroom. Every time a group leaves the class for an intervention the appropriate sheet goes with them. The TA uses the sheet to record absences so that any issues can be swiftly addressed and on each occasion will refer to the sheet and discuss the targets with the pupils, thereby ensuring that they are fully aware of what they are trying to achieve and are constantly reminded of why they are there and not in the classroom. Progress towards the targets is noted and shared with pupils who are consequently encouraged and motivated. Any issues regarding progress, behaviour or inappropriate placement in the group are recorded – not at length: short bullet points suffice – and when the sheet is returned to the file in the classroom, if any comments have been added, the TA will place a post-it note on the outside of the folder or file so that the class teacher is alerted. In a secondary school I have seen similar documentation held by the Provision Map Leader in the maths department and used to provide feedback to teachers during, and at the end of the period of intervention.

Any system that a school sets up should be easy to maintain, and the teacher should use the resulting documentation when evaluating the impact of the interventions. Schools that use electronic Provision Mapping systems should check whether such an option is available on the system or whether they will need to create their own.

Schools must make every effort to establish whether the way that interventions are being delivered is having a positive impact and determine this as early on in the programme of delivery as possible. For instance, a pupil's absence from the intervention should always be challenged, as should any obvious inappropriate grouping, either for reasons of behaviour or for reasons of ability. I recently observed a fairly large group of pupils accessing a reading intervention where one pupil was extremely disruptive whilst 'waiting his turn'. My conclusion was that the group was too large to be effective – too much time was lost to sitting and waiting; and he was wrongly placed – when he started to read it was obvious that he was reading at a far higher level than the other members of the group.

In such an instance the teacher should be alerted to this by word of mouth, email or through use of the intervention record sheet, and should swiftly adjust the group, not wait for the end of the period of intervention. Where timetabling clashes are revealed, action should be swiftly taken and the Provision Map should be adjusted accordingly.

Do Provision Maps help us to find out what works?

The Provision Map can be seen as a tool to support Action Research. The decision about which interventions should be delivered in a school should always be made in light of national and local research as well as through consideration of what has worked in the school in the past. Where a school has established that an intervention has been successful in enabling pupils to achieve the targets set for them then it is right that the interventions should be repeated. However, where interventions are not proving successful the school must find an alternative.

Comprehensive research into the impact of interventions can be found in the Sutton Trust/Education Endowment Fund's Teaching and Learning Toolkit (http://educationendowmentfoundation.org.uk/toolkit/) and, in the fourth edition of his report into which literacy interventions have greatest effect, Professor Brooks reports on 57 different schemes for the improvement in literacy outcomes and concluded the following:

- Ordinary teaching ('no treatment') does not enable children with literacy difficulties to catch up.

   o *Implication: Although good classroom teaching is the bedrock of effective practice, most research suggests that children falling behind their peers need more help than the classroom normally provides. This help requires coordinated effort and training.*

- Schemes for KS3 are few, but several work well for reading, and Grammar for Writing has great potential.

   o *Implication: Provided they receive continuing support, children who make these gains should be better able to cope with the secondary curriculum.*

- Schemes for children who struggle with spelling work best when highly structured.

   o *Implication: Children with spelling problems need schemes tailored to their preferred ways of learning and delivered systematically 'little and often'. Such schemes work particularly well for enabling children to grasp relatively regular patterns of spelling.*

- Work on phonological skills for reading should be embedded within a broad approach.

   o *Implication: Phonics teaching should normally be accompanied by graphic representation and reading for meaning so that irregular as well as regular patterns can be grasped. Children with severe difficulties in phonological skills, or using English as an additional language, may need more 'stand alone' phonics teaching to support their speaking and listening.*

- Children's comprehension skills can be improved if directly targeted.

   o *Implication: Engaging the child in exploring meaning embeds the relevance of reading for life, expands vocabulary and broadens the range of texts. Children falling behind their peers need both carefully structured reading material and rich, exciting texts.*

- ICT approaches work best when they are precisely targeted.

   o *Implication: The mediation of a skilled adult is essential to ensure technologically driven schemes meet children's needs. Time needs to be allocated effectively so that the diagnostic tools of programmes can be used for each child appropriately.*

- Large-scale schemes, though expensive, can give good value for money.

  o *Implication: When establishing value for money, long-term impact and savings in future budgets for special needs must be considered, particularly when helping the lowest-attaining children.*

- Where reading partners are available and can be given appropriate training and support, partnership approaches can be very effective.

  o *Implication: Reading partners need skilled training and support to maximise impact. A school needs to manage partners so that feedback to classroom teachers is effectively and regularly given. Teaching assistants (TAs) and learning support assistants (LSAs) are well equipped to undertake this role.*

- Good impact – sufficient to at least double the standard rate of progress – can be achieved, and it is reasonable to expect it.

  o *Implication: If the scheme matches the child's needs, teachers and children should expect to achieve rapid improvement. High expectations are realistic expectations in most cases.*

(Brooks 2013, p. 18)

One of the key roles for SENCOs (senior leaders in special schools) in the Provision Mapping process is to keep their colleagues informed about interventions that are proven to be effective. In my view, the SENCO's workload is becoming increasingly unmanageable and often a SENCO's own professional development is sacrificed to attendance at the numerous meetings that their role demands. I believe that each school should ensure that the SENCO has sufficient time to familiarise themselves with current theoretical and practical guidance for the teaching of SEN pupils and also has the opportunity to share that with colleagues. The ongoing professional development of all staff is a critical feature in the effectiveness of teaching in any school. Opportunities should be provided for all staff to become familiar with new strategies and interventions, for the dissemination of training and the sharing of what works on a regular basis.

Checklist for Do

In place in our school?	Yes	No	Needs developing
Provision Maps detail how often a pupil is absent from class to attend interventions.			
Teachers make use of guidance on effective strategies to improve their teaching.			
There are timetabled opportunities for staff to share good practice.			
We get good value for money from training.			
The appraisal cycle is linked to the Pupil Progress Review cycle and thus able to influence the setting and review of teachers' targets.			
Our support staff are being set appropriate pupil progress targets as part of their appraisal.			
We share intervention targets with pupils so that they understand what they are expected to achieve.			
Intervention record sheets are used to record key data for each intervention and as a simple system for sharing information between TA and teacher.			
We keep abreast of new developments/research so that we can find alternatives for any intervention that is insufficiently effective.			

Chapter 5

Review

All effective schools will have an established methodology for assessing and reviewing pupil progress. It will incorporate review of progress in class and will also be linked to reporting to parents and other stakeholders on the effectiveness of its actions. The most effective schools monitor pupil achievement constantly through the use of the many and varied forms of formative assessment. But they also timetable key points for review to swiftly follow assessment opportunities, and use this review opportunity to monitor the impact of the additional provision and to plan for next steps. Ofsted's review of SEN and disability reported that:

> Inspectors saw the similar needs of different children being met effectively in a wide range of different ways. However, what consistently worked best was a close analysis of their needs, often as they changed and developed, matched to a clear view of the impact of intervention on outcomes for them.
>
> (Ofsted 2010c, p. 10)

The Code of Practice emphasises that the 'impact and quality of the support and interventions should be evaluated' (SEND, Jan. 2015, para. 6.54) and also refers to the scrutiny Ofsted will make of SEN provision:

> As part of any inspection, Ofsted will expect to see evidence of pupil progress, a focus on outcomes and a rigorous approach to the monitoring and evaluation of any SEN support provided.
>
> (SEND, Jan. 2015, para. 6.72)

Reflection on progress in interventions needs to be rigorous. Howes and colleagues (2009) found that uncritical discussion or ill-informed reflection on inclusion can sometimes reinforce inappropriate action. Schools should honestly consider:

- whether they are continuing to deliver a programme or intervention that they have been using for years simply because they have that programme and the people trained to deliver it;
- how many programmes are dropped when it is shown that they have little or no impact;
- how many Pupil Progress Review or departmental meetings actually bring about change to practice or intervention.

In order to ensure that change happens there needs to be a structure to enable informed reflection and critical discussion on progress in interventions and in class. This can be achieved through regular Pupil Progress Review conversations which incorporate a review of interventions, but all must be expertly led and given a high priority in order to be effective.

The SEND Code of Practice explains how critical pupil and parental involvement in review of the intervention is:

> Parents should have clear information about the impact of the support and interventions provided, enabling them to be involved in planning next steps.
> (SEND, Jan. 2015, para. 6.55)

and

> the school should readily share this information with parents. It should be provided in a format that is accessible (for example, a note setting out the areas of discussion following a regular SEN support meeting or tracking data showing the pupil's progress together with highlighted sections of a provision map that enables parents to see the support that has been provided).
> (SEND, Jan. 2015, para. 6.75)

I believe that if schools adopt the system of Provision Mapping that I recommend then they will be able (on one document) to review the impact of interventions, make strategic development decisions and plan next steps as well as demonstrate all of this to parents and other stakeholders.

Questions that will be answered in this chapter:

- Who should evaluate Provision Maps?
- How often should teachers review interventions?
- How can Pupil Progress Review meetings be used to greatest effect?
- How can pupils and parents be involved in the review of interventions?
- How can SENCOs use Provision Maps to collate and share information with other agencies?
- How should SENCOs evaluate the impact of interventions across the school and use that information effectively?
- How could school leaders use Provision Maps to evaluate Pupil Premium spending?

Who should evaluate Provision Maps?

I want to stress that it is not the SENCO's responsibility to evaluate the Provision Map; the SENCO's role is to collate all of the information from the various Provision Maps and demonstrate impact across the school. The review phase is not a stand-alone phase; teachers will be constantly gathering evidence as part of formative assessment. Even though the gathering of pupil and parent views will not always take place at a predestined time, this information will be gathered in a number of ways, the school will need to timetable regular review opportunities. *In all phases it should be the teacher who carries out the initial review of interventions.* This is vitally important as it means that teachers are required to consider the progress of their pupils when they are away from the classroom. It helps to reinforce the teachers' responsibility for their pupils' progress at all times and will help them determine whether the intervention is having impact that is sufficient in each case to merit the pupil's absence from the classroom. Such practice is emphasised in the Code of Practice.

> The class or subject teacher, working with the SENCO, should revise the support in light of the pupil's progress and development, deciding on any changes to the support and outcomes in consultation with the parent and pupil.
>
> (SEND, Jan. 2015, para 6.54)

If the class teacher or subject teacher has set a suitably SMART target at the outset of the intervention, it will be a simple matter for them to consider whether those targets have been met or not. Schools have often encountered problems when measuring small steps of progress with such crude measures as National Curriculum sub-levels, bands or grades. I believe it is inappropriate for schools to rely on the somewhat dissociated in-class assessment data. I have already explained that the method I recommend is to place the emphasis on ensuring the intervention target is SMART enough when it is set. If that has been achieved, and any entry and exit data is related to the target, the teacher should be able to easily ascertain whether the intervention target has been met or not.

However and whenever the formal review of interventions takes place, the school must prioritise the review of interventions if it is going to get the best possible outcome. Time needs to be set aside for teachers and support staff to plan together, but also to review together. This should be a timetabled opportunity and should be used to make regular checks on appropriateness of target, intervention design, grouping, timetabling, etc. Through this ongoing process intervention should be adapted to better meet the needs of pupils and impact should be increased.

A very experienced primary school SENCO has this advice to share with schools. I think her recommendations about the impact of teachers and support staff working together to regularly review interventions would be of use in secondary and special schools as well.

In my experience, Provision Maps become a more dynamic and impactful document when the class teacher and teaching assistant meet regularly (perhaps fortnightly) to discuss them. The difficulty is always whether a timetable slot can be prioritised in order for this to take place.

The benefits I have seen are:

1   Class teacher becomes aware of how the intervention is running – attendance issues, behaviour, resource concerns as they arise and so immediate action to improve can be taken.
2   As the teacher and TA discuss the interventions, it becomes clear what is working in a small group, what is being learnt, and so within the class this can become a focus for the adults to ensure those skills are transferred. This can work the other way too – blocks within class learning can be discussed and added to intervention targets.
3   Well-being and involvement are often higher in small group settings, these discussions can result in trialling similar strategies for whole class settings.

When Teaching Assistants are given shared ownership of the Provision Map and involved in their regular review, the result is a dynamic document that has greater impact. If TAs don't use the Provision Map as part of their daily practice, it is more likely to sit in a drawer and be brought out at a pupil progress meeting for evaluation when it is already too late to make any different arrangements.

(Rowena Banks, SENCO, Sevenoaks Primary School, Kent)

In some commercial systems there is little or no emphasis on the evaluation of provision, only a record that it has taken place. Each of the commercial companies will have developed system-specific features, for instance the Provisionmapwriter system from Blue Hills (Figure 5.1) notes which teacher has set up the intervention and sends them an e-mail reminder when it is time to review it. I think this feature would be particularly useful in the secondary phase.

As the member of staff responsible for setting up the intervention will need to evaluate whether the target has been met or not, it should have been written by them in such a way that it is SMART, and therefore measurable enough, to allow accurate evaluation. At the point of formal review of intervention I encourage school staff to evaluate the interventions their pupils access in such a way that they can record the proportion of pupils who have met the target in the appropriate column as well as record any comments on the effectiveness of the intervention and/or its delivery, to support decisions about whether the intervention should be repeated or not. This will help SENCOs to evaluate the impact of all of the interventions without having to track back through all of the intervention record sheets and this will be explained more fully in the phase-specific Chapters 6–8.

How often should teachers review interventions?

This is a difficult question to answer as the frequency of review may need to vary somewhat according to the interventions provided. For instance, schools generally assess pupil progress a minimum of three and maximum of six times per year. In some instances, reviewing the impact of an intervention could only take place once the intervention programme has been completed, which may be a period of time out of sync with the school's assessment calendar. In other cases, the intervention may

Additional provision from: 06/09/14 to: 22/07/15

Lennon Oliver   Year group: 7   Teacher/Tutor: Miss L Hyde

Intervention type	Intervention	Staff involved	Sessions per week	Session length (mins)	No. of weeks to run	Start	Finish	£	Hrs	Target achieved?
Literacy	Booster Units	Mrs. G Ball, HLTA Mrs. C Craig, TA Level 1	10.0	30	2	08/10/14	14/10/14	£48	10	W
In class support	Learning Support	Miss Z Marshall, TA Level 2	5.0	60	25	08/10/14	20/04/15	£625	125	Yes
							Totals:	£673	135	
							Grand totals:	**£673**	**135**	

Figure 5.1 Provisionmapwriter: pupil and interventions record, academic year 2014–2015

be on-going, and therefore its effectiveness should be assessed as regularly as pupil progress is determined. Whatever the period of review, it should be established at the outset so that the measurement of whether the target has been met or not within a pre-determined interval is the indicator of success. I think that some schools have an anxiety about reviewing after too short a period, as they believe that impact could not be measured. I think there is no such thing as reviewing too soon or too often, as it is always better to consider the appropriateness and success of an intervention in an on-going fashion that will enable swift changes to be made should they be required. Interim assessments would indicate whether the intervention is being successful and for very short-term interventions a subsequent assessment would measure whether impact has been sustained over time.

How can Pupil Progress Review meetings be used to greatest effect?

The correct vehicle for in-school discussion about the effectiveness, or otherwise, of interventions is the Pupil Progress Review meeting (primary and special) or the departmental meeting (secondary). The Pupil Progress Review conversations conducted during these meetings play a vital role in the evaluation of the effectiveness of classroom teaching strategies and the interventions carried out, as well as providing an opportunity for collaborative planning for next steps. This will be true in all schools, though the meetings may appear somewhat different in different phases. I believe the essential elements of any successful Pupil Progress Review conversation to be common to all phases and every school should be explicit in its instruction to staff on the expectations of them in this regard. Such expectations could be incorporated into a school's teaching and learning policy. For instance:

- All teachers will complete their analysis of pupil progress and provide the SLT/ head of department with a copy of the analysis in the week prior to the meetings.
- The SLT/head of department will analyse the data and prepare questions about pupil performance that the teacher will be prepared to answer.
- Teachers will consider which teaching (Wave 1) strategies have been successful and why, as well as those that have been less successful, and be prepared to discuss this.
- The impact of any intervention undertaken since the last pupil progress meeting will be discussed and the evidence used to plan new interventions.
- Teachers will consider which pupils are in need of additional intervention in the coming term, decide what form that should take as well as set SMART intervention targets and draft a new Provision Map (primary) or contribute to the drafting of a Provision Map (secondary).

What should the meeting look like?

I am often asked what a good Pupil Progress/departmental Review meeting looks like. I think it is helpful to think of the meeting in sections.

Part I

The first part of the conversation (about 20 per cent) should be centred on the review with some key questions:

- Who has made good progress, and who has not?
- Are there are any groups that have performed better than others?
- Are there any other factors such as attendance and behaviour that need to be taken into account?

If teachers know that only 20 per cent of the time will be devoted to this area, it may help them to understand the importance of carrying out a full analysis in advance of the meeting so that discussion of these aspects is brief and focused.

Part 2

In order to maximise impact, the majority of the time in the meeting should be spent on answering the 'so what are we going to do about it?' question. The discussion about what action to take is critical and should be focused primarily on what adjustments need to be made to classroom teaching. This should include:

- a review of the strategies that have proved successful as well as those that have not;
- whether there are any different strategies that could be used;
- if necessary, where a teacher could go to for support or training.

The aim is that teachers will have spent some time considering their own strengths and weaknesses and should come to the meeting prepared to share this information so that their strengths can be disseminated and their weaknesses addressed and improved. If teachers have not been able to self-reflect in this way, the SLT/ department lead should use the information they have about the quality of teaching alongside the analysis of pupil progress and evaluation of interventions and may need to engage in a robust conversation around improvement at another suitable opportunity. In the SEN review Ofsted endorses this emphasis on the need for quality in whole-class teaching rather than additional intervention:

> Inspectors observed schools focusing on providing additional help for pupils with identified special educational needs rather than on improving the quality of their standard offer for all pupils. In some of their visits to schools, inspectors met pupils who were provided with significant additional support whose needs could and should have been met by appropriately differentiated teaching, good learning and pastoral support earlier on.
>
> (Ofsted 2010c, p. 22)

In total, the discussion about teaching strategies should take up a further 40 per cent of the meeting time.

Part 3

Only once the discussion about classroom teaching strategies has concluded should there be any discussion about interventions. This section will absorb the final 40 per cent of the meeting time. Again, the meeting will be expedited by good preparation on the part of the teachers (the Provision Mapping Leader in secondary English or maths department) who should have evaluated the impact of the interventions on the Provision Map prior to the meeting. The following questions could then be posed:

- What does the evaluated Provision Map tell us works best?
- Should any interventions be continued?
- Should any interventions be ceased or replaced with something more effective?
- Should any grouping or timetabling issues be addressed?

Final progress meetings: transition

The final Pupil Progress Review meeting of the year should be a transition meeting. It would be sensible to ensure that teachers from the current class and teachers of the next year's class are involved in the review meeting so that the new teacher can be apprised of the range of needs in the class and the interventions and strategies that have been successful in meeting those needs. This will reduce the number of meetings in a school if the Pupil Progress Review meeting and the transition meeting are combined. It also means that the teachers can work together to plan a draft Provision Map for the new class and that intervention can commence as soon as the new school year starts.

How can pupils and parents be involved in the review of interventions?

One of the chief aims of the changes to the SEND Code of Practice was that pupils and their parents should become more involved in the provision that is made for them by schools, health teams and social care. In school there are many ways that the views of pupils and their parents could be gathered and recorded. Many primary and special schools use pupil passports to communicate information about how pupils prefer to learn and strategies that must, or should, be used to engage them. I am grateful to Claire Garrett, the SENCO at Warden House Primary School, for sharing the resource she has created (Figure 5.2).

Such documents generally raise pupil and parent confidence in the ability of the school to understand their needs and therefore to meet them well. The passports are sometimes retained by the pupils themselves and used by them to communicate their preferences to adults they don't feel confident enough to talk to. In special schools they can be vitally important where pupils cannot communicate verbally and where their safety could be compromised because of their disability. The way that parent views are linked to the pupil views gives the document greater validity and helps parents to better understand how their child presents to teachers in school. In secondary schools they sometimes have the opposite effect; although I have seen it used very

I like: Bananas, my friend Child B, holding Blue Tac, sitting next to my Teacher, my dog Bob **I don't like:** Assembly, gravy and wet things on my dinner, paint on my hand and writing	**I am really good at:** Numbers, running fast, listening to stories, being a good friend **Parent comment:** *Child A will count to 10 repetitively and this shows anxiety – she will need to be given a distraction. We enjoy bed time stories and I am pleased she has a friend* **Teacher comment:** *Child A can retell and sequence stories really well*
What I find difficult: Sitting still, not getting angry, writing, sometimes I don't listen **Parent comment:** *We need to repeat instructions twice, and make them short. Writing homework is a struggle* **Teacher comment:** *Child A is making progress with her writing however it can be scribed at home so there is less anxiety*	**When I am grown up I want to:** Work with dogs and ride a horse **Parent comment:** *I didn't know Child A liked horses, we might look at riding lessons* **Teacher comment:** *We will use horses to link into written work and reward systems*
This will help me learn (resources, strategies, time, adults): I like pictures showing me what to do and someone to help me **Parent comment:** *Child A needs to work on listening and calming down, visuals and countdowns help at home* **Teacher comment:** *Countdown sticker help in class – see individual resources in class. Child A needs to have an adult to support but she is also working on her independence*	**Other things that help me/support me:** Don't talk to me when I am cross, help me with my shoelaces, I can show you when I am sad and happy with my pictures **Parent comment:** *Child A can do her shoelaces and doesn't need help! We are using the sad and happy faces at home and she is getting better at using them.* **Teacher comment:** *Child A has time out space*
I would like you also to know: I am learning to use my face cards (5 Point Scale). I need to take my jumper off when I am too hot **Parent comment:** *If Child A gets too hot behaviour can become an issue – I am pleased she has recognised that she needs to be aware of this.* **Teacher comment:** *We will monitor this in class and make lunchtime supervisors aware*	**Parent/carer signature** Date................................... Signature............................... Date................................... Signature............................... Date................................... Signature...............................
<u>Resources:</u> **Visual timetable** **5 Point Scale** **Red cards (for additional adult support)** **Happy/sad faces** **Visual time countdown**	<u>Behaviour management:</u> **BMP in place** **Time out space** **SLT adult support when required**

Health:	Outside agency support:
Asthma pump in medical basket – blue cupboard	Paediatrician Speech and Language Therapist

Other:

Be aware of over-heating

Child A can have a snack and drink when de-escalating from behavioural incident

Use visual timetable and 5 Point Scale

Figure 5.2 Pupil passport

effectively, some children feel stigmatised by being asked to carry round such a document. I feel that it is the duty of the school to determine whether a pupil would prefer to use such a document or not before imposing it on him or her.

One of the most critical features of successful intervention is that the pupils engage with this additional provision. If a pupil is reluctant to attend, or cannot see the point of accessing intervention that takes him or her away from the classroom, then the success of the intervention may well be limited. Class teachers need to gather pupil views on the additional intervention and add this information to their evaluation of the outcome of the provision. This does not need to be in a formalised, quantitative way; for example, it is not necessary to use questionnaires or surveys. The views of pupils should be collected principally through conversation and observation. Most teachers are well aware of pupils who are hesitant or reluctant to leave the classroom to attend an intervention and most are aware of those who engage with additional intervention with obvious enthusiasm. But there often needs to be a further examination of these responses. The class teacher will want to know whether the grouping is working for the pupil; the only girl in a group of boys might be struggling; social issues that may have arisen during break time could affect the mix of Year 7 girls in an intervention and the wrong mix of ability can be very problematic. The timetabling issues also need unpicking; is the child missing a favourite lesson or an area of the curriculum in which they excel, to go to an intervention group that is a continuation of the very thing he or she has struggled with for half of the morning?

These 'soft' data are critical when it comes to assessing the impact of the intervention and when planning for further intervention. I would suggest that at some point during the intervention period, and not just at the very end, the views of pupils are sought and recorded on the intervention record sheet. The person most suited to conducting this conversation will vary – it could be the teacher, it could be the person delivering the intervention or another member of the school staff. The information could also be augmented by comments from parents or other pupils. The information collected in this way should be used by teachers to contribute to their evaluation of the impact of any intervention, and any specific issues raised during the Pupil Progress Review meeting so that appropriate action can be considered by the teacher in consultation with the support staff, senior leaders and the SENCO.

The need to improve parental confidence in a school's actions to meet the needs of pupils with SEN was first highlighted in the findings of the Lamb Inquiry (2009), which, in turn, influenced many of the recommendations found in the Green Paper *Support and Aspiration: A New Approach to Special Educational Needs and Disability*. In this paper, the government pledged to reform education and health provision for pupils with special educational needs and to build parental confidence that schools are able to meet their child's needs (DfE 2011b). It is critical for a school to share information with the parents of its most vulnerable pupils in such a way that they will easily understand the provision being made for their child and have confidence in those delivering it. The Code of Practice guides schools to provide parents of pupils with SEN the opportunity to meet with staff and discuss provision at least three times per year. I suggest that the most appropriate way of sharing the Provision Map with parents in the primary phase is for the class teacher to anonymise the draft Provision Map and share it with parents during a parent consultation meeting and in secondary schools for teachers to share information about interventions during their consultation events. Such a recommendation is echoed in the SEND Code of Practice where it describes how schools should involve parents and pupils in planning and reviewing progress:

> Where a pupil is receiving SEN support, schools should talk to parents regularly to set clear outcomes and review progress towards them, discuss the activities and support that will help achieve them, and identify the responsibilities of the parent, the pupil and the school. Schools should meet parents at least three times each year.

> These discussions can build confidence in the actions being taken by the school, but they can also strengthen the impact of SEN support by increasing parental engagement in the approaches and teaching strategies that are being used. Finally, they can provide essential information on the impact of SEN support outside school and any changes in the pupil's needs.

> These discussions should be led by a teacher with good knowledge and understanding of the pupil who is aware of their needs and attainment. This will usually be the class teacher or form tutor, supported by the SENCO. It should provide an opportunity for the parent to share their concerns and, together with the teacher, agree their aspirations for the pupil.

> Conducting these discussions effectively involves a considerable amount of skill. As with other aspects of good teaching for pupils with SEN, schools should ensure that teaching staff are supported to manage these conversations as part of professional development.

> These discussions will need to allow sufficient time to explore the parents' views and to plan effectively. Meetings should, wherever possible, be aligned with the

normal cycle of discussions with parents of all pupils. They will, however, be longer than most parent-teacher meetings.

The views of the pupil should be included in these discussions. This could be through involving the pupil in all or part of the discussion itself, or gathering their views as part of the preparation.

A record of the outcomes, action and support agreed through the discussion should be kept and shared with all the appropriate school staff. This record should be given to the pupil's parents. The school's management information system should be updated as appropriate.

(SEND, Jan. 2105, paras 6.65–6.71)

How to share Provision Maps with parents will be described more fully in Chapters 6–8 which describe the phase-specific Provision Mapping systems. The consultation with parents should not be too one-sided though, it must include information gathering as well. Parents have a wealth of information about their children to share with schools that may well help teachers to select and use the most appropriate strategies and interventions to meet pupil needs.

How can SENCOs use the Provision Map to collate and share information with other staff and other agencies?

There will be a need to share the class Provision Map with a range of other staff. For example, where pupils are accessing an intervention for English, all subject teachers will need to be aware of this – and of the target for the intervention – so that support can be cross-curricular. Supply teachers, student teachers, temporary staff or volunteers will need to be made aware of the strategies in place to meet the needs of all pupils, as well as the range of interventions being provided and their timetabling. Members of the SLT may want to use the Provision Map when carrying out observations of teaching to determine what impact the teaching strategies listed on the Provision Map have on learning behaviour etc. The school must ensure that whatever system it uses, commercial or school-based, the Provision Maps must be accessible to all who need to use them and yet remain confidential from those that do not.

The school may also need to use the Provision Map to demonstrate the action it has taken to meet the needs of a pupil for whom they are seeking external agency involvement or statutory assessment. In such cases, and when needing to provide evidence to Ofsted of the impact of the school's action on a pupil with SEN, or a pupil who is in receipt of additional funding (Pupil Premium), the school may wish to use a case study approach. In this pro-forma the school is able to demonstrate the barriers to learning and how those barriers have been, and are, being addressed (Figure 5.3). A current Provision Map or Provision Plan attached to this would support the documentation.

If the school is preparing for an Ofsted inspection and wishes to prepare a number of case studies in readiness, I suggest that a case study is produced for one pupil from each of these groups: SEND, Pupil Premium, Child in Care (CiC), High Achiever, and any other vulnerable groups the school has identified/is supporting – for instance, pupils from traveller families, summer-born, etc.

	Reading	Writing	Maths
Pupil			
Yr/class			
Vulnerable group (including SEN level and dimension)			
Pen picture			
Prior attainment data			
Current attainment			
End of year targets			
End of Key Stage targets			
On track? Yes/No			
Attendance history previous year/current			
Behaviour/exclusion history Previous year/current			
Bullying incidents			
Current provision and timetabling (evidenced on Provision Map and/or Provision Plan) and evidence of impact			
Eligible for High Needs Funding Y/N details			
External agency involvement			
Pupil views			
Parent views			
Comments			

Figure 5.3 Pupil case study document

In every school the SENCO will be responsible for collating the evidence necessary to access external agencies such as speech and language therapists, physiotherapists, educational psychologists, etc., and for requests for statutory assessment. It will therefore be the SENCO who will be responsible for providing evidence to the LA of impact of provision made over time and who will provide data of provision made over time to support transition to another school. The evaluated Provision Maps can provide the information required and are now often requested by external agencies who value the ability to consider the intervention that has been accessed by this pupil in a class or whole school context. However, it may be complicated to look back over many maps to catalogue all of the interventions a pupil has received over several years and so in some cases, I suggest the school augment this with an individualised record of the intervention accessed over time. All of the commercial systems I have looked at have this facility and if a school uses such a system it will be easy to print off a record of intervention accessed over many years, but this will not necessarily give any information other than what was offered. It will not answer any queries about impact. Whether your school is using such a system or not, I believe it is easy, using the information from each class Provision Map, to build up a log of interventions accessed which, in this instance, does not need to be an evaluative exercise, merely a pupil-level record that serves to indicate the number and range of interventions which have been necessary to achieve the progress that has been made (Figure 5.4).

An updated copy of this log may be kept by the SENCO. This record would be a useful document to support transition and would also be a way for the SENCO to quickly track whether any pupil has been accessing a worryingly high number of interventions. In the example shown, the SENCO may well be concerned about Mary Smith, but should be able to reconcile this hard data with the class Provision Map, the conversations in Pupil Progress Review meetings, the observations of teaching in the class and in the interventions, and be confident that this high level of intervention is appropriate and necessary to ensure that progress is satisfactory. However, if the SENCO were concerned that this high level of intervention was having a negative impact upon Mary's progress or well-being, it would be a starting point for discussion with the class teacher and could indicate the need for a pupil case study to determine what her needs are and whether they are being met appropriately.

An evaluated Provision Map can support requests for additional support from outside agencies, as it can demonstrate that a range of approaches and intervention have been provided and what impact they have had. It can demonstrate, for example, that an intervention that has been highly successful for most pupils has not had the same impact on the identified pupil; that an alternative intervention was attempted but that this too failed to secure the accelerated progress achieved by other pupils, and that therefore there should be further assessment or investigation of the needs of this pupil and possibly a statutory assessment. Because all the targets are SMART, the progress towards them will be relevant. If the targets have been created in such a way that the outcome is clearly measurable, there should be no problem for outside agencies being able to understand school-specific assessment language. Targets from external agencies such as speech and language therapists or physiotherapists can be entered on to and evaluated on the Provision Map for individuals. This action will

Interventions (Term attended)	ELS	FLS	SALT	Physio	Maths	Toe/toe	Phonics	Social skills						
Pupil														
Joe Bloggs		1		3				1						
Mary Smith			123	123	123	123	123							
John Brown														
Amy Green					2		123	123						

Figure 5.4 Intervention log

mean that the class teacher has a better understanding of the needs of those pupils and how best to meet them.

How should SENCOs evaluate the impact of interventions across the school and use that information effectively?

The evaluated Provision Map contains evidence of the impact of the interventions over the previous period of intervention. This information should have been shared by the class teacher with the SENCO and SLT before the Pupil Progress Review meeting, but it needs to be reflected upon further to support the school's strategic prioritisation of resources and staff. The effectiveness of each intervention must be considered and this information should be used to help the class teacher (or Provision Mapping Leader) determine:

- whether to continue or discontinue it;
- whether it should be extended to make provision for more or larger groups of pupils;
- whether it should be delivered in a different way;
- whether it should be delivered over a different length of time or at a different time of day.

It should be used by the SENCO to determine:

- whether there are any staff training needs that should be met to secure the greater success of a programme.

Conversely, where an intervention has been extremely successful, the SENCO should consider:

- whether it can be used more widely throughout the school;
- whether it could be shared with other schools in the locality.

If those delivering the interventions have performance appraisal targets that are linked to intervention targets then the evaluated Provision Map can be used to support their review. This may also support decisions about whether they need to access further training and development.

If all of the Provision Maps are collated and the impact of provision across the school is evaluated by the SENCO this information can be used to support the school's self-evaluation and reported to governing bodies and to Ofsted (Figure 5.5). This table shows a condensed version of such a document (some of the columns have had to be reduced so that the document could be reproduced) and gives an idea of how challenge could be made to the impact of interventions.

The evaluation of impact of interventions across the school is vital. It allows the school to determine where there are areas for development and any identified training needs can be added to the school development plan and budgeted for, along with the purchase of any resources needed to support efficient delivery. It helps the school to

Table: Effectiveness of interventions whole school Term 2 2014 2015

Class	Literacy – 1:1 daily reading %	n	Literacy – BRP %	n	Literacy – reading recovery %	n	Literacy – comprehension/ inference %	n	Literacy – writing %	n	Literacy – handwriting %	n	Literacy – phonics letters and sounds %	n	Literacy – high frequency words %	n	Literacy – spelling %	n	Literacy – precision teaching %	n
6 Lion	0%	2	100%	1			50%	4	0%	3										
5 Leopard	25%	4	33%	3			25%	4	40%	5									75%	4
4 Tiger	75%	4					83%	6	100%	6									0%	2
4 Woodpecker	0%	3	100%	3					0%	6										
3 Hedgehog	100%	3	100%	2					50%	6										
2 Squirrel	17%	6	100%	1	50%	2	100%	2	83%	6									0%	2
2 Goldfinch	0%	8	0%	1					67%	6									0%	2
1 Badger	100%	2	100%	1															100%	3
1 Nightingale	25%	8	100%	2									0%	1						
Average	47%	79	79%	21	50%	2	61%	31	61%	119	33%	13	0%	1	100%	4	88%	8	42%	23

Figure 5.5 Overview of effectiveness of interventions in a primary school showing % met target and number accessing intervention, by class

swiftly and appropriately bring about change to pupil support and ensure that 'value for money' is being achieved. Value for money is a measure of whether accelerated progress has been achieved in the time allocated for the intervention. This information will be required when evidencing the impact of any High Needs funding from the LA.

Ofsted judges schools on the impact of the interventions to support pupil progress, and in the *School Inspection Handbook* (current at time of writing) states that 'inspectors will consider the progress that lower-attaining pupils are making and the impact of provision for them on raising their attainment' (Ofsted, June 2015, para. 176). From September 2012 when inspections started to be carried out with minimal notice, schools have been expected to provide evidence of self-evaluation to inspectors as they commence their inspection. With so little time to prepare for inspection, the information to inspectors needs to be provided in a succinct and easy-to-interpret format and should preferably be available on the school's website. I suggest that a table such as that in Figure 5.5 would demonstrate the impact of interventions and would be particularly valuable to inspectors, enabling them to swiftly identify strengths and weaknesses that could reinforce or discount theory of an appropriate inspection trail. If the school were to summarise the evaluation of impact of interventions and prepare a statement for the school self-evaluation document that supports the overview of interventions, the text would explain any anomalies. A SENCO from a primary school describes how she evaluates all the interventions across her two site school and shares that information with governors.

Eastchurch Church of England Primary School is a larger than average school which is split over two sites. It is now a two form entry primary school that takes up to 472 children from the ages of 3 to 11 years. The two sites are approximately 3 miles apart. Both sites have been using Provision Mapping for around two years. The system has now evolved to include additional data required for Pupil Progress Reviews such as Pupil Premium information and attendance. Following Pupil Progress Reviews, class teachers write new Provision Maps. I attend Pupil Progress meetings when requested and advise on appropriate interventions. When assessing children at the end of a term, class teachers evaluate their maps. I then take the evaluated maps and assess the impact of interventions across year groups, by site and across the school as a whole. On the impact statement I include how many children are in each group in order to offer context for the success/failure of the intervention. The impact statement raises questions which are discussed when this information is shared with SLT, literacy and numeracy co-ordinators and the SEN Governor. The SEN Governor will share the information with the governing body. We also share specific impact information with parents at parent/teacher meetings and also as evidence for access to other services such as speech and language therapy and to inform paediatricians. In addition, successful interventions are recommended to other schools through our Local

(continued)

(continued)

Inclusion Forum discussions. In school we use the information to decide whether groups should continue; if an intervention is particularly effective we consider whether to use it for other children in other year groups, if it is not effective we look for alternatives and it helps us to review timetabling for staff. Additionally, it allows us to identify training needs for those delivering the interventions. Assessing the impact of interventions also allows us to illustrate where we are targeting areas for school improvement.

(Juliette Ede, SENCO,
Eastchurch CofE Primary School, Kent)

How could school leaders use Provision Maps to evaluate Pupil Premium spending?

There is often a high correlation between pupils identified with SEN and those eligible for Pupil Premium or Pupil Premium plus (for Children in Care (CiC) or children recently adopted from care). Schools know their pupils well and can identify this 'overlap' easily but must be even clearer about the impact of all the additional funding that is being accessed by each child. The needs of this sub-group of SEN and Pupil Premium will possibly make them the most vulnerable pupils in the school. The Provision Map, and especially the evaluation of interventions, can be used to demonstrate the impact of Pupil Premium at a group or individual level quite easily.

If all interventions that are funded through Pupil Premium are highlighted in some way on the Provision Map, we can quickly and easily see the impact of those interventions on the pupils accessing them. Highlighting individuals would enable a comparison to be made between the performance of Pupil Premium and non-Pupil Premium pupils not just in the school's assessment data but also in the impact of interventions. It would also allow the school to quickly and easily monitor its impact on that most vulnerable group, SEN/PP.

Some commercially available Provision Mapping systems, for instance Pupil Asset, provide the school with a whole school analysis of intervention and from this the SLT, governors or Ofsted could draw conclusions about the effectiveness of all the interventions across the school. This particular analysis shows the cost per session so that the school can consider the value for money of the provisions it offers and it also shows where the provisions can be funded through Pupil Premium (darkest shading). This feature allows the school to determine the gap between Pupil Premium funded interventions and non-Pupil Premium funded interventions (Figure 5.6).

Schools may wish to use a simple table to demonstrate the effect of Pupil Premium funding on eligible pupils in the six key areas; attendance, reading, writing, maths, behaviour and enrichment (Figure 5.7). Such a resource, updated each year, would demonstrate how the school has used funding to best effect to narrow the gap and could also be used to demonstrate planned next steps. It could be used by governors to challenge the impact of any funding and to determine whether the school has correctly identified areas for spending in the coming year.

Provision Map | Overview

Provision Map | Provision Map Overview

DISPLAY OPTIONS

Date Range: └ 2014: Autumn pt1 ⬍

04/09/2014 → 22/10/2014

[Refresh]   [Reset Display Options]

Provision Map Overview	After School Club £20 p/h	hearing impaired £20 p/h	After School Catch Up £35 p/h	Football Tuesdays £12 p/h	Intervention Plus £40 p/h	A to O dyslexia support £30 p/h	Saturday Club £80 p/h	Intervention 101 £100 p/h	provision demo £40 p/h
Year 6	50%	N/A	100%	75%	87%	0%	N/A	N/A	0%
Year 5	N/A	0%	75%	0%	N/A	75%	50%	N/A	N/A
Year 4	0%	0%	100%	N/A	N/A	50%	N/A	0%	0%
Year 3	N/A	N/A	N/A	N/A	N/A	100%	N/A	0%	N/A
Key Stage 2	33%	0%	88%	60%	67%	42	100%	0%	0%
Year 2	N/A	N/A	50%	N/A	N/A	N/A	N/A	N/A	0%
Year 1	N/A	N/A	N/A	N/A	N/A	100%	N/A	N/A	N/A
Key Stage 1	N/A	N/A	50%	N/A	N/A	100%	N/A	N/A	0%
Reception	N/A	N/A	N/A	N/A		N/A	N/A	N/A	N/A
N2	N/A	N/A	N/A	N/A		N/A	N/A	N/A	N/A
N1	N/A	N/A	N/A	N/A		N/A	N/A	N/A	N/A
Key Stage 0	N/A	N/A	N/A	N/A	N/A	N/A	N/A	N/A	N/A
Total	33%	0%	80%	60%	67%	46%	50%	0%	0%

(Tooltip near Key Stage 2 / Saturday Club column: "Group contains Pupil Premium")

Figure 5.6 Pupil Asset overviews of interventions including Pupil Premium

Pupil Premium analysis

	CIC	Adopted from Care	Ever 6	FSM	Services	Other
Academic year			**Total received**		**% school roll PP**	
No. pupils						
Pupil Premium/ non-Pupil Premium	Attendance %	Reading (in-year pts progress)	Writing (in-year pts progress)	Maths (in-year pts progress)	Behaviour incidents	
	Lateness %	Reading attainment	Writing attainment	Maths attainment	Exclusions (days)	
Action taken and cost						
Impact						
Next steps						

Figure 5.7 Pupil Premium analysis tool

Checklist for Review

In place in our school?	Yes	No	Needs developing
Teachers evaluate interventions.			
The targets are SMART enough to evaluate easily.			
Teachers are fully aware of their responsibilities in preparing for Pupil Progress Review.			
Pupil views are collected and acted upon.			
Parents understand the interventions in place for their child and how they can support their child.			
Provision Maps are shared with support staff, temporary staff, volunteers, etc.			
Even though we share the Provision Map, we maintain confidentiality.			
Evaluated Provision Maps are used to support requests for support or statutory assessment.			
Evaluated Provision Maps are used to calculate the impact of interventions across the school.			
This information is shared with governors/LA/Ofsted in an easy-to-read format.			
Our evaluation of intervention helps us evaluate the impact of Pupil Premium funding.			

Chapter 6

What should Provision Mapping look like in primary schools?

Whatever system is used, in a primary school the class teacher should be the person responsible for the class Provision Map and it should be they who draft, maintain and evaluate it. The aim of this (in line with Teachers' Standards and the SEND Code of Practice of 2015) is to increase the responsibility of class teachers for all pupils in their class (including those with SEN) at all times – even when the pupils are absent from the classroom attending additional intervention. The reason that I believe Provision Mapping can help the class teacher understand the responsibility they have for any additional provision is best illustrated by the SENCO and class teacher of a primary school in Kent which operates a school-based, non-commercial system. The practice in this school has travelled a long way from its starting point just over two years ago, to a position where the class teachers themselves run pupil progress meetings and lead on the drafting and review of Provision Maps, using them as essential classroom management tools:

> We began to adopt Provision Mapping in late 2012. The importance of accurate assessment and data analysis, and the links with Pupil Progress Review meetings lay at the core of the concept. Provision Mapping has helped monitor interventions for all children and the deployment of TAs and additional teachers and has been further developed so that it now aids in the tracking of pupil premium children and the evaluation of related resourcing.

> Following an Ofsted inspection which highlighted concerns, a process of regular school improvement visits by the local authority and our own self-evaluation has meant the school has swiftly moved through stages of development to achieve a far better way of monitoring and evaluating additional provision. Data is analysed six times a year by both SLT and class teachers during Pupil Progress meetings, and used to plan provision and interventions. This is, in turn, linked to whole school target setting and target setting for pupils, as well as informing staff appraisal targets.

> Provision Mapping has led class teachers to take real ownership of their classes, in terms of assessment, analysing data, developing interventions, setting targets, deploying support staff and running Pupil Progress meetings. The changes made – through rigorous action planning that addressed the issues from the Ofsted judgement – have had a particularly positive impact on the perception of teachers towards their responsibility for SEND (just in time for the new

Code of Practice). Feedback from Pupil Progress meetings and staff appraisals have shown increased confidence in supporting children with SEND and low achievers. As a result, interventions have become highly focussed and are now reducing in numbers as Teachers and TAs have become more confident about meeting needs within the classroom through enhanced quality first teaching.

(Nigel Cates, SENCO and Assistant HT,
West Minster Primary School, Sheerness West Federation, Kent)

The use of the Provision Map has allowed me to become more focused on the actual development target the children required. I have found that having the SMART target aimed at a particular child or group of children has enabled evidence to be gathered on even the smallest steps of progress that a child has made which, for the lower attaining children, is very important indeed. With regular and frequent evaluation of the target I can eliminate the risk that a child not making progress within an intervention would be overlooked for too long and allows me the flexibility to include a child in an intervention group that will benefit them mid term if necessary. Provision Maps help me to effectively manage intervention for children of all levels of ability; they allow areas of development to be identified and give a clear plan to address how to give children the skill to learn and thrive in their learning.

I feel that the Provision Map is very much a working document, evidencing what the children need, showing the progress that they have achieved over the period and also highlighting the next steps in their learning journey. They have become very beneficial within the class, being a resource that is used and contributed to by all adults within the classroom. They are used to ensure that the interventions taking place are effective for each individual child and we can use them to demonstrate the good rate of progress the interventions achieve.

(Tina Ovenden, Class Teacher,
West Minster Primary School, Sheerness West Federation, Kent)

As described above, we can see that where the system is used to best effect it is used as a tool for managing the provision that a teacher deems necessary.

Schools' growing reliance on electronic, web-based systems to record and track pupil information means that many are tracking and analysing pupil progress more swiftly and accurately and have sophisticated analysis tools at their fingertips. As mentioned in earlier chapters, some of the systems now incorporate Provision Maps, but there needs to be careful consideration of whether those system-based Provision Maps have all the properties of the optimum Provision Mapping system that I described in Chapter 3 and the primary model I describe in this chapter. If your school has purchased a commercial system to track pupil progress you will expect it to be accurate, reliable and able to analyse the data you input in many different ways. If you also want that system to support effective pupil progress tracking it will need to:

- link to the school's Management Information System (MIS) and update pupil information daily;
- analyse or RAG (Red, Amber, Green) progress so that those falling behind can be easily identified;
- identify pupils eligible for additional funding (Pupil Premium, etc.);
- identify pupils with SEN Support and/or with an EHC Plan;
- identify SEN pupils by need type.

If that same system has a Provision Mapping facility you should consider whether it encourages the *teachers* to:

- identify pupils in need of intervention;
- construct intervention groups;
- set targets for interventions;
- set the frequency and duration of interventions and make any necessary adjustments mid-intervention (for instance the adjustment of groups or targets);
- add pupils (and staff) to interventions;
- evaluate the impact of the interventions against whether the target has been met or not;
- generate reports for parents.

Schools should also reflect on whether the system they have bought into allows the SENCO to:

- obtain an overview of the interventions in place across classes, year groups and across the school;
- calculate costs for each intervention and for each pupil;
- identify where interventions could be funded through Pupil Premium;
- obtain a whole school evaluation of the impact of the interventions that identifies any that are insufficiently effective.

Such a system would meet the needs of many schools but I am not sure that every school would be able to achieve all that they want from it. In the remainder of this chapter I will describe a Provision Mapping system that any primary school could use to manage the interventions it provides. This is the same system that I described in my earlier book *Provision Mapping: Improving Outcomes in Primary Schools* with a few adjustments to take account of changes under the new SEND Code of Practice.

Drafting the Provision Map

The process of Assess, Plan, Do and Review is cyclical and so it is hard to determine where it actually starts. However, the action to address any inadequate pupil progress or attainment will always start with assessment. In earlier chapters in this book I have outlined the process for assessing pupils, analysing data and gathering pupil views. Once the class teacher has a very clear idea of who is making good progress and who is not he/she should consider strategies and interventions that would be most effective to redress any inadequate progress and the pupils who need to access them. From this the teacher should create a draft version of the class Provision Map for the coming term. In a primary school a class Provision Map should appear as in Figure 6.1.

Primary school: class Provision Map

Class:　　　　　　**Intervention start date:**　　　　　　**Intervention review date:**

Quality first teaching strategies:

Intervention	Group size	Frequency/staff	Pupil	Entry data	Target/outcome (SMART)	Exit data	Impact	Proportion target met

Figure 6.1 Draft primary school Provision Map

Date: Each Provision Map should be dated and the class identified so that the teacher who holds responsibility and the period of intervention is clear (Figure 6.2).

Teaching strategies: The teacher should update the teaching strategy box with those strategies that are necessary to meet the needs of the class at that time (Figure 6.3). This is a critically important feature of a class Provision Map for this is the place where any information on the regularly used strategies will be listed. Such information will help remind teachers to use the strategies, help cover staff to meet pupil needs and help parents to understand all the ways in which their child is supported.

Timing, frequency, duration and staffing: As you will see from this draft version of a class Provision Map, the teacher has entered the groups and interventions proposed for the coming term (Figure 6.4). The group size has been entered (important if pupils are being drawn from more than one class for interventions and also important when calculating cost), as has the timing, frequency, duration and the person delivering the intervention. This particular feature of the Provision Map enables the teacher or SENCO to calculate the time a pupil spends away from the classroom and I have often found it to be extremely valuable. In one school I used the Provision Map to track an individual pupil selected at random. The child was absent from the classroom for a total of five hours per week. The length of time he was absent from the classroom never exceeded 20 minutes and I estimated that he must be absent for a part of nearly every lesson. When asked about his behaviour it was little surprise to hear that he found it difficult to settle and concentrate in lessons. Teachers must reflect on the total length of time their pupils are absent from lessons and ensure that any absence from the classroom is absolutely essential. It also allows support staff to be identified which will give the school an idea of cost.

Entry data: Entry or baseline data should be entered alongside pupil names, but it must be relevant to the target.

Intervention targets: Targets that are SMART enough to be measurable must be considered and written on to the Provision Map (Figure 6.5). The targets are the most important feature of any Provision Map and the teacher should ensure they are **SMART,** in particular, that they are **Specific** enough to be easily **Measurable.**

- **Specific:** The class teacher will have devised targets that relate either to gaps in learning or to developing skills hitherto undeveloped.
- **Measurable:** This should be clearly evident (but does not need to rely on testing).
- **Achievable** (but also **Aspirational**): Achievable should, in my view, be joined by Aspirational. Many schools question whether accelerated progress can be made in interventions, but research tells us that we should expect that it can be.
- **Relevant:** The class teacher will have set the targets from a gap analysis and from what is known about the child as well as with regard to current in-class targets and aspects to be covered in schemes of work.
- **Timed:** The targets will remain pertinent for the duration of the Provision Map.

Primary school: class Provision Map

Class: Swallows Intervention start date: 09-09-14 Intervention review date: 16-12-14

Quality first teaching strategies:

Intervention	Group size	Frequency/staff	Pupil	Entry data	Target/outcome (SMART)	Exit data	Impact	Proportion target met

Figure 6.2 Primary school Provision Map, dates

© 2016 Provision Mapping and the SEND Code of Practice, Anne Massey, Routledge

Primary school: class Provision Map

Class: Swallows

Intervention start date: 09-09-14

Intervention review date: 16-12-14

Quality first teaching strategies:

Visual timetable, task boards x 5, peer mentoring, grouping for support, cumulative reward system, writing frames, word banks, feelings wall, worry box, phone-a-friend, wobble seats x 3.

Intervention	Group size	Frequency/ staff	Pupil	Entry data	Target/outcome (SMART)	Exit data	Impact	Proportion target met

Figure 6.3 Primary school Provision Map, teaching strategies

Primary school: class Provision Map

Class: Swallows Intervention start date: 09-09-14 Intervention review date: 16-12-14

Quality first teaching strategies:

Visual timetable, task boards x 5, peer mentoring, grouping for support, cumulative reward system, writing frames, word banks, feelings wall, worry box, phone-a-friend, wobble seats x 3.

Intervention	Group size	Frequency/staff	Pupil	Entry data	Target/outcome (SMART)	Exit data	Impact	Proportion target met
Writing group	1:6	3 x 30 x 4 weeks **HLTA** (Mrs C)	**Amy** **Joe** **Dan** **Fred** **Bob** **Max**					
Numeracy	1:6	4 x 20 x 8 weeks (early am) **HLTA**	Dan Fred Carl Amy Jane Sara					
Paired reading	1:1	Daily, x 10, **HLTA**	Joe					
Social skills	1:3	3 x 15 per week	Carl Jack **Wayne**					

Figure 6.4 Draft primary school Provision Map, frequency and duration

Primary school: class Provision Map

Class: Swallows Intervention start date: 09-09-14 Intervention review date: 16-12-14

Quality first teaching strategies:

Visual timetable, task boards x 5, peer mentoring, grouping for support, cumulative reward system, writing frames, word banks, feelings wall, worry box, phone-a-friend, wobble seats x 3.

Intervention	Group size	Frequency/staff	Pupil	Entry data	Target/outcome (SMART)	Exit data	Impact	Proportion target met
Writing	1:6	2 x 60 x 6 weeks HLTA (Mrs C)	Amy Joe Dan Fred Bob Max		To be able to write in complete sentences. To be able to use marking ladders to self check punctuation successfully.			
Numeracy	1:6	4 x 20 x 8 weeks (early am) HLTA	Dan Fred Carl Amy Jane Sara	Test score/20 10 7 7 9 4 7	To be able to use multiplication facts (2,5 and 10) confidently To use the 24 hr clock			
Paired reading	1:1	Daily, x 10, HLTA	Joe	RA (Accuracy) 6.3	To re-engage with text Read with expression			
Social skills	1:3	3 x 15 per week	Carl Jack Wayne	Leuven 1 2 4 2 3 2	To work on targets Organisational skills Working with others Working with others			

Figure 6.5 Draft primary school Provision Map, entry data and targets

If the targets are sufficiently SMART the entry and exit data columns may well be left unused. The targets must be written using not only the formative assessment data but also the views of the pupils and parents, and in language that pupils and their parents can understand.

In an ideal world, the teacher would share the draft Provision Map with senior leaders and the SENCO at the Pupil Progress Review meeting. All at the meeting would discuss the interventions proposed and would agree that proven effective interventions have been selected with appropriate frequency of delivery. The Provision Map would then be agreed and the period of interventions commenced. However, in reality not all staff attend Pupil Progress Review meetings this well prepared. In some schools the Provision Map is drafted at the review meeting and in some schools it is drafted following the meeting.

Maintaining the Provision Map

Once finalised, the draft Provision Map becomes a working document. The teaching strategy box may be used by the teacher as a reminder of strategies that have proved to be effective in this class or in other classes, recently or at other times. The teacher can refer to this section of the Provision Map when planning learning activities and when determining groupings, etc. It could also be used by members of the SLT when carrying out observations of teaching and learning to determine whether the teaching strategies discussed and advised on during a Pupil Progress Review meeting are in place and fully embedded in daily classroom practice. For example, is a visual timetable in place and regularly referred to by pupils, thus indicating that it is part of normal classroom practice? The information in this box is also of significant importance to any supply teacher engaged to teach the class, as it provides evidence of the strategies pupils will expect to see in place and will support continuity and consistency if the regular teacher is absent.

It is not necessary to wait until the end of an intervention period to update a Provision Map. As the term progresses the teacher should update the Provision Map to show changes to teaching strategies where some have proved unsuccessful and others have been added, and to groups, frequency and timings of interventions as necessary. The best Provision Maps are those that are regularly scribbled on, adjusted and amended. If a pupil is experiencing a problem in a group, if the timetabling of a group is causing difficulties, if the frequency of the intervention sessions needs to be increased, adjustments should be made before the end of the intervention period and any changes recorded on the Provision Map.

Sharing Provision Maps with parents

The use of regular parent consultation opportunities to share information about the interventions is recommended in the SEND Code of Practice. Such action ensures that parents understand that any additional intervention will not be something completely separate from the learning their child will be engaged in in the classroom, whilst at the same time reassuring them that action is being taken to meet their child's needs. I have found that optimum timing for these consultation events to be as soon as possible after Pupil Progress Review meetings so that the teachers are discussing recent assessments and can share a draft Provision Map with parents at the start of a period of intervention.

I believe it is important to share the Provision Map with *all* parents irrespective of whether or not their child is accessing additional intervention. This will help parents understand that at any point in their time at the school their child may need additional intervention, but that will not necessarily mean they will have SEN. The way I would do that would be to put the class Provision Map on to the interactive whiteboard in the classroom where the discussion is taking place and also to put it on the school's website in the relevant class or year group area or page. The teacher can then use it to demonstrate to those parents whose children are not currently having additional intervention how the quality teaching strategies named on the Provision Map might be supporting their child. One reason for including entry data on the draft Provision Map if it is relevant to do so is that it will enable the class teacher to explain to parents how pupils are identified for additional intervention and why their child does, or does not, need to access any at this particular time.

The anonymisation of the Provision Map is critical if we are going to share it with parents. In Figure 6.6 we see how a draft Provision Map should be anonymised before it is shared. The column of names is blanked out so that individuals cannot be identified. Other aspects of the Provision Map should also be removed before the document is shared with all parents. For instance the 1:1 reading with one pupil would mean that the pupil would be easily identified. This is not an issue as all children in the class will be aware that this is going on, but his reading age score should not be public knowledge and therefore should be removed (Figure 6.7). Likewise, the social skills intervention should not be shared publicly (nor would it be wise to identify any interventions such as counselling or anger-management, etc.) and so should be blanked out in the same way that pupil names are (Figure 6.8).

For parents of pupils who are identified for intervention, the Provision Map can be very reassuring. They can understand how the intervention groups are composed and why their child needs to access them. They can also see how often and for how long the intervention will be delivered. If the intervention is to be delivered before or after school there can be a conversation about the need for punctuality or any clashes with out-of-school activities. Through discussion about the intervention targets, parents can be helped to understand how to support their child at home and what they should expect to see in terms of progress if the intervention has been successful. Parents of pupils who have had intervention which has now ceased can be reassured that it has ceased because the target has been reached and can remain confident that rigorous monitoring of their child's progress will be ongoing. Through the use of the whiteboard the school can avoid the costly printing of Provision Maps, but I would have some available if any parent wants a copy to take away with them.

The following case study illustrates the benefits of sharing Provision Maps in this way and it is my experience that parents generally favour such comprehensive information over the more personalised information they would have received in an IEP.

Primary school: class Provision Map

Class: Swallows **Intervention start date: 09-09-14** **Intervention review date: 16-12-14**

Quality first teaching strategies:

Visual timetable, task boards x 5, peer mentoring, grouping for support, cumulative reward system, writing frames, word banks, feelings wall, worry box, phone-a-friend, wobble seats x 3.

Intervention	Group size	Frequency/ staff	Pupil	Entry data	Target/outcome (SMART)	Exit data	Impact	Proportion target met
Writing group	1:6	3 x 30 x 4 weeks HLTA (Mrs C)			To be able to write in complete sentences To be able to use marking ladders to self check punctuation successfully			
Numeracy	1:6	4 x 20 x 8 weeks (early am) HLTA		Test score/20 10 7 7 9 4 7	To be able to use multiplication facts (2,5 and 10) confidently To use the 24 hr clock			
Paired reading	1:1	Daily, x 10, HLTA		RA (Accuracy) 6.3	To re-engage with text Read with expression			
Social skills	1:3	3 x 15 per week		Leuven 1 2 4 2 3 2	To work on targets Organisational skills Working with others Working with others			

Figure 6.6 Primary school Provision Map, anonymised, 1

Primary school: class Provision Map

| Class: Swallows | | Intervention start date: 09-09-14 | | | Intervention review date: 16-12-14 | | | |

Quality first teaching strategies:

Visual timetable, task boards x 5, peer mentoring, grouping for support, cumulative reward system, writing frames, word banks, feelings wall, worry box, phone-a-friend, wobble seats x 3.

Intervention	Group size	Frequency/staff	Pupil	Entry data	Target/outcome (SMART)	Exit data	Impact	Proportion target met
Writing group	1:6	3 x 30 x 4 weeks HLTA (Mrs C)			To be able to write in complete sentences To be able to use marking ladders to self check punctuation successfully			
Numeracy	1:6	4 x 20 x 8 weeks (early am) HLTA		Test score/20 10 7 7 9 4 7	To be able to use multiplication facts (2,5 and 10) confidently To use the 24 hr clock			
Paired reading	1:1	Daily, x 10, HLTA						
Social skills	1:3	3 x 15 per week		Leuven 1 2 4 2 3 2	To work on targets Organisational skills Working with others Working with others			

Figure 6.7 Primary school Provision Map, anonymised, 2

Primary school: class Provision Map

Class: Swallows **Intervention start date: 09-09-14** **Intervention review date: 16-12-14**

Quality first teaching strategies:

Visual timetable, task boards x 5, peer mentoring, grouping for support, cumulative reward system, writing frames, word banks, feelings wall, worry box, phone-a-friend, wobble seats x 3.

Intervention	Group size	Frequency/staff	Pupil	Entry data	Target/outcome (SMART)	Exit data	Impact	Proportion target met
Writing group	1:6	3 x 30 x 4 weeks HLTA (Mrs C)			To be able to write in complete sentences To be able to use marking ladders to self check punctuation successfully			
Numeracy	1:6	4 x 20 x 8 weeks (early am) HLTA		Test score/20 10 7 7 9 4 7	To be able to use multiplication facts (2,5 and 10) confidently To use the 24 hr clock			
Paired reading	1:1	Daily, x 10, HLTA						

Figure 6.8 Primary school Provision Map, anonymised, 3

Whilst discussing the implications and changes of the new SEND Code of Practice with a group of parents, I suggested the idea of class teachers sharing Provision Maps during the 3 meetings throughout the school year with them. (Anne had made the suggestion of trying this on a recent course I had attended.) The parents felt that this would be really useful as they would be able to see the programmes that the school/class are able to offer, in addition to what is available day to day in the classroom. This may include literacy, numeracy and behaviour programmes to support children's learning. By sharing these at parent consultation evening with each of the pupils' parents, we have been able to explain which intervention is being used, tell them how long it will last and what progress we are expecting their child to make. We will then meet with parents at the end of the intervention period to discuss progress. We ask the parent/guardian of a pupil with SEN to sign a copy that can be retained at school in their SEN file and the parent takes a copy away with them. The parents have felt very well informed and it has helped to iron out confusions over the variety of interventions that we deliver in school.

(Ruth Palmer, SENCO, Charing C. E. Primary School, Kent)

However, not all schools like this approach and many prefer to share personalised information about the intervention their child is in receipt of with parents. Such practice would meet the needs of the parents by keeping them informed, but would not enable them to see the provision their child is receiving in context with the rest of the class, something many parents find very reassuring.

Evaluating the Provision Map

At the end of the intervention period the Provision Map needs to be evaluated. This will be achieved by considering whether the target for the intervention has been met or not (Figure 6.9). The teacher may need to make reference to the intervention record sheets and/or other datasets such as attendance and behaviour records.

If a school is both assessing and reviewing pupil progress six times per year, the end of the intervention period will coincide with the Pupil Progress Review meetings and the exit data will always be current and relevant. However, for those schools assessing pupils six times per year but only reviewing progress four times per year, the end of the intervention period will not necessarily coincide with the Pupil Progress Review meetings. This has been known to create a dilemma for some schools: when and how to enter the exit data for interventions on the Provision Map? For instance, in a school that assesses and reviews three times per year, an intervention that runs for six weeks will end before the end of the school's assessment interval. How should the outcome of the intervention be recorded in such an instance? As I have previously made clear, this system is intended to reduce bureaucracy and so I would advise that the teacher judge whether the target has been met or not at the end of the predetermined period of intervention and record that on the Provision Map at the same time. A true measure of impact is whether any progress gained through the provision of

Primary school: class Provision Map

Quality first teaching strategies:

Visual timetable, task boards x 5, peer mentoring, grouping for support, cumulative reward system, writing frames, word banks, feelings wall, worry box, phone-a-friend, wobble seats x 3.

Intervention	Group size	Frequency/ staff	Pupil	Entry data	Target/outcome (SMART)	Exit data	Impact	Proportion target met
Writing group	1:6	3 × 30 × 4 weeks HLTA (Mrs C)	Amy Joe Dan Fred Bob Max		To be able to write in complete sentences. To be able to use marking ladders to self check punctuation successfully		All met targets except Joe – behaviour an issue. Two sessions missed	5/6
Numeracy	1:6	4 × 20 × 8 weeks (early am) HLTA	Dan Fred Carl Amy Jane Sara	Test score/20 10 7 7 9 4 7	To be able to use multiplication facts (2,5 and 10) confidently. To use the 24 hr clock	Test Score/20 20 10 17 10 17 20	Good progress. Positive outcome for all in use of 24 hour clock. Fred still stuck on 5 ×. Amy attendance poor	4/6
Paired reading	1:1	Daily, × 10, HLTA	Joe	RA (Accuracy) 6.3	To re-engage with text. Read with expression	RA (Accuracy) 7.2	Good progress 1:1 – this works better for Joe and should be extended	1/1
Social skills	1:3	3 × 15 per week	Carl Jack Wayne	Leuven 1 2 4 2 3 2	To work on targets. Organisational skills. Working with others. Working with others	Leuven 3 3 4 4 4 4	Leuven well-being and involvement improved. Carl needs task board at all times	3/3

Figure 6.9 Primary school Provision Map, evaluated

additional intervention is sustained, therefore teachers could record level of attainment (or whether target has been met) at the point of cessation of intervention, and then again at the next assessment point. If the exit data column is split in two and dated, both data could be recorded and the teacher could demonstrate whether any initial gains have been sustained or built on.

Whatever the pattern of assessment and review, before each Pupil Progress Review meeting, all exit data should be entered on to the Provision Map and the impact of the intervention determined by the class teacher in preparation for that meeting. A copy of the evaluated Provision Map should be provided for the SLT and SENCO to consider in the week prior to the Pupil Progress Review meeting. This will enable the school to build up a clear picture of 'what works' and so be able to disseminate that information to other teachers during the Pupil Progress Review meetings and be best placed to consider alternatives to any unsuccessful interventions.

The teacher's review of the impact of interventions needs to be very rigorous in order to ensure that the intervention in place is effective enough. The Ofsted SEN review noted that 'even where assessment was accurate, timely, and identified the appropriate additional support, this did not guarantee that the support would be of good quality'. Further into the review it is reported that:

> Inspectors found that weaker providers did not always evaluate their own provision rigorously enough to identify whether what they were providing for individual pupils was sufficiently effective.
>
> (Ofsted 2010c, p. 40)

The evaluation of impact of intervention will be supported by a range of information other than hard assessment data. Pupil views should be considered at this point: have any of the pupils commented that the behaviour of other pupils in the intervention group was a barrier to learning? Were there issues of timetabling or grouping? Information can also be gathered from the intervention record sheets (Figure 4.1): have there been a number of occasions when the intervention did not take place? The class teacher should also consider attendance and behaviour data and record any individual or group issues in the impact column so that the evaluation of the intervention is complete. The quality of the class teacher's evaluation of the Provision Map will impact on the SENCO's ability to evaluate the impact of interventions across the school.

Checklist for Provision Mapping in primary schools

In place in our school?	Yes	No	Needs developing
Provision Maps drafted by class teachers.			
Provision Maps show the key data including targets and entry and exit data.			
Intervention targets are SMART.			
The Provision Map helps teachers track pupil absence from the classroom.			
Class Provision Maps are evaluated by class teachers.			
Intervention record sheets are used to record key data for each intervention and as a simple system for sharing information between TA and teacher.			
Interventions are prioritised and the number of interventions in place is reducing over time.			
Anonymised Provision Maps are shared with parents in such a way that they understand the provision their child is receiving and how they can help at home.			

Chapter 7

What should Provision Mapping look like in secondary schools?

In wanting to find efficient ways to track and evaluate the additional and different interventions they provide for their pupils, secondary schools are no different from primary schools. Although I have been successfully using Provision Mapping to achieve this with primary schools for many years, a suitable secondary system seems to have been difficult to establish. Over the last year or so I have seen huge improvements in commercial Provision Mapping systems and now believe that these provide secondary schools with the best solution to managing and evaluating their additional provision. However, I am aware that not all schools will want or be able to afford a commercial, web-based system and so I will share the departmental approach to Provision Mapping that I have found to be most effective in secondary schools to date.

From all the work that I have done, I believe that what secondary schools want from any Provision Mapping system is:

- the ability to know what additional interventions are being delivered across the school by all of the departments and whether they are effective enough;
- whether pupils have met targets set for the interventions and if not, why not;
- the ability to quickly and easily produce a list of additional interventions for any one pupil so that they can evidence impact of additional funding.

In a secondary school, the success of a Provision Mapping system will depend on the same critical features of a successful primary system.

There must be:

- easy-to-access information about students and strategies that work for them;
- accurate analysis of assessment data that can identify stalled or inadequate progress;
- frequent discussion about progress and how to address any that is not good enough through the enhancement of classroom teaching;
- regular discussion about 'what works' in the classroom;
- understanding of which interventions are most effective;
- clear and relevant target setting derived from gap analysis or formative assessment;
- regular review of the impact of the strategies and intervention that informs the 'what works' conversation.

In a primary system the responsibility for all additional intervention sits easily and obviously with the class teacher. In a secondary school there must be a corporate responsibility for the progress of all pupils, yet there is sometimes more abdication of responsibility by teachers for pupils with additional needs than there is in the primary phase. In the new curriculum and assessment arrangements (Progress 8 and Attainment 8) there will be greater cross-referencing of pupil progress between subject areas which I believe should enhance corporate responsibility. But it is just as important in this phase that staff see the provision of additional and different intervention as integral to all that the school provides to help its pupils achieve their targets. Interventions should be closely linked to the curriculum currently being taught so that all learning is relevant and regularly reinforced.

Many of the secondary schools with whom I work have used staff development time this year to introduce teachers to the changes in the new SEND Code of Practice, and I have seen teacher awareness of SEN improve as a result. But secondary schools need to harness this improvement and drive change still further by ensuring that teachers are aware of, and using, classroom strategies to support pupils with SEN. Although in primary and special schools I recommend using the Provision Map to enhance teacher awareness of the strategies that improve the learning experience of vulnerable pupils, I do not think that this can sit alongside the monitoring and reviewing of interventions in a secondary school in quite the same way. I know that SENCOs in secondary schools spend considerable time collating information for teachers and sharing it with them, only to be frustrated when it becomes apparent that not all teachers take notice of or use the information to improve their teaching. All secondary schools will want their system of information sharing to work well but in this instance I think such an information sharing system can sit alongside the Provision Map instead of embedded within it, as in the primary system. However, I do think that teachers need to play a larger part in determining and evaluating additional interventions.

My experience of working with secondary schools tells me that almost all have established and sophisticated systems for recording and tracking pupil progress. The assessment information that is entered on to these systems needs to be accurate for them to be reliable. Secondary schools often use current grade and/or predicted grade to measure attainment (particularly in KS4). Every school should be making on-going and regular checks on the accuracy of the assessment information so that the precision of current and predicted grades can be validated and moderation should be an embedded and frequent activity.

As long as the data is accurate, these systems (whether they have a Provision Mapping facility or not) should enable teachers to identify pupils whose progress is stalled or inadequate and should allow any attendance at extra intervention to be recorded. Any system would be enhanced by the facility to identify when the pupils with stalled or inadequate progress are provided with an additional intervention and would be even further enhanced if their progress data were flagged to identify this (a very basic form of Provision Mapping). However, such automated systems are sometimes difficult to navigate; they are data-driven (rather than target-driven) and seldom involve teachers in the creation of intervention groups. Secondary teachers do not always set the targets for interventions, as their primary colleagues do, yet it is they who have carried out the formative assessment; they who know the gaps in learning and therefore it is they who have knowledge of the targets that should be prioritised.

Because no two secondary schools operate in the same way and so many different staff teach each pupil, it is understandable that there are logistical barriers to the establishment of a single model of secondary Provision Mapping. But the 2015 SEND Code of Practice makes no distinction between primary and secondary education – it simply recommends Provision Mapping as a useful tool. If the principles are the same and the expectation is that Provision Mapping could be used in a secondary school – what should it look like and how should it be managed?

Just as in primary schools, there are two options – to use a commercial, web-based progress tracking system with a Provision Mapping facility, or to create a simple school-based system to be used alongside the school's data tracking system.

A secondary SENCO, relatively new to post, describes the school-based system he has designed for use in his school. As we will see, communication and sharing of information is highly developed and effective, but teachers are not as involved as they could be in setting and evaluating interventions:

The SEN register is an electronic document that appears as a short cut on every member of staff's PC. Students are listed by year group, and the register includes the student's need type, further comments and details from the SEN department as well as comments from parents and students regarding specific strategies which teachers should employ/avoid etc. In addition, at the top of the SEN register are hyperlinks to general information and recommended teaching strategies (bullet points) for teachers to employ for the main need types in the school. These documents are a maximum of 2 pages long so are brief but accessible.

For students with more complex needs an individual IEP is produced. This includes much more detail regarding the student's needs and issues surrounding this. In addition to strategies recommended by parents and the student themselves, teachers add comments of things that they find work well or should be avoided with individual students. This is very detailed and personal and includes tips such as the student's favourite football team. All of this helps to build relationships between student and teacher and enables good practice to be shared through a consistent approach.

All students in the school are listed on the Provision Map, regardless of SEN/PP, etc. Each year group has its own tab. Interventions are added with the following information: Intervention programme; Subject; Staff; Group size; Term; Academic year; Frequency (Total weeks; Sessions per week; Minutes per session); Entry test level; Intervention programme targets; Exit test level; Target achieved; Outcome / Future action.

Determined to improve the engagement of teachers in its use, the SENCO goes on to say:

Currently this information is only used within the SEN department for tracking, to inform planning, to monitor the core offer and for applications for external support. However, the intention is that the system will be better used across the school in order to empower teachers in the ability to meet the needs of the

SEN students in their classes, as well as to suggest appropriate interventions for particular individuals.

(Keir Williams, SENCO, Wrotham School, Kent)

In another secondary school a commercial system is being used to good effect. This Provision Mapping facility is apparently more successful in engaging staff in setting targets for interventions as well as in their assessment and review.

Provision Mapping at the Folkestone Academy

The AEN (Additional Educational Needs) register is linked to SIMS and developed as a SIMS AEN mark sheet which for each student has academic data, attendance information, CAT and reading scores, a brief student profile, a summary of the strategies and interventions already used for that student and lastly a note of all documents attached to SIMS for further reference and detail as to how to support the students, for example diagnoses or reports from STLS or SALT. Teachers have this information on their mark sheet for each of their teaching groups. A hard copy of this is kept in every class planner, which they refer to and annotate on a day-to-day basis as ongoing assessment happens in the classroom. This continuous evaluation of the most effective in-class strategies to ensure that each student can make progress means that information can be fed back by teachers to be added onto the central AEN mark-sheet which is regularly updated. In this way teachers take responsibility for quality teaching strategies.

When a teacher identifies that a student may need further additional assessment or support they make an AEN referral, which, in our school is via a tracked email, linked system. They are then asked to complete an audit tool to demonstrate what has already been provided for this pupil and the impact. They can do this simply by referring to their own annotated class planner sheets and so are happy to do this to support a referral for additional support.

The school reviewed several options for mapping additional SEN and PP interventions having previously found recording and evaluation of Provision Maps complicated to fully coordinate, write up and keep up to date manually. Having trialled several IT based solutions, the one found to best meet the needs of the secondary phase at the school was Provisionmapwriter by Blue Hills which is fully coordinated with SIMS, taking automatic weekly updates.

Provisionmapwriter is a secure web based system; every member of staff has their own login and password and can input their own SEN or PP intervention details to which they add the students they are working with. They input information about the intervention such as start, end and review dates; length of session, frequency and who is involved; the aims of the intervention, how it will be reviewed and the intended outcomes. They then also input the start levels and targets for each student added to the intervention. When review of the intervention is due, the system sends a reminder email to that member of staff who then

(continued)

(continued)

adds an update of information about each student's progress and engagement in the intervention. At the end of the intervention they will evaluate whether the student has achieved the target, is working towards or has not achieved it, also whether the student had full attendance at the intervention.

Those with administrator or manager access to the system in our school are the SENCO and a member of SLT overseeing Pupil Premium allocation who can view financial data hidden from other users. We can generate Provision Maps instantly by pulling together all of the information added in by every different person delivering interventions across the year. Individual student Provision Maps can be produced which give full overview about all the different interventions a student has had, or is receiving, and their progress within these. These are ideal for sharing with parents at review meetings and building students' profile information.

In addition a fully costed individual Provision Map can also be produced instantly for each child as staff cost and budget data is all updated within the system. This is invaluable for evidence to support application for High Needs funding. A full range of further data evaluation about the provisions made for any of the cohorts within the school can be produced instantly for SLT reporting, planning and evaluation purposes.

When we introduced Provisionmapwriter to the school, we delivered a thirty minute training session to key staff that could then cascade this to others. In addition to this basic training, prior training had been given about choosing the right tools to measure various aspects of progress, for example the use of Leuven scales for measuring well-being and engagement with learning, other tools included the Boxall Profile system as well as self-evaluation scales, behaviour scales and communication and interaction scales. A session on writing SMART targets was also delivered to all staff. We held further training on reviewing interventions as soon as all staff had successfully set theirs up and reviews have now taken place.

This Provisionmapwriter system was introduced only two terms ago but is now fully used by all staff. There have not been any real teething problems and we have already been involved in advising another secondary school in its introduction. We have used the printed reports to support several EHCP applications. Where the student's individual Provision Maps have been used in meetings with parents, they have been very pleased with how clearly they can understand all of the interventions and their child's progress within them. The greatest advantage to the strategic management of additional provision and evaluation is that all teachers and support staff take responsibility and ownership for keeping information about their intervention updated and accurate which shares the workload and makes it manageable whilst enabling and improving accurate scrutiny by SENCO and SLT. It will also be useful for individual staff when providing evidence for their performance management reviews. Feedback from all staff using the system has been positive.

(Cathy Aldritt, SENCO and Head of AEN,
The Folkestone Academy)

Commercial web-based Provision Mapping system

There are many commercially available systems such as that described by the SENCO from Folkestone Academy. I have not listed or described them all, nor have I recommended one over another, as by the time this book is published there will be new versions of almost any system on the market today. However, my research has led me to conclude that the simpler they are the more they will be used. Many of the web-based systems currently available require significant additional data entry, which means that they are time-consuming and teachers' reluctance to use them could be raised. If any school is currently considering the purchase of a web-based universal progress tracking system with a Provision Mapping facility built in, it should establish whether it has the properties required to meet its needs. I suggest it consider the following checklist

Does the universal pupil progress tracking system:

- link to the school's Management Information System (MIS) and update pupil information (attendance, behaviour, assessment) daily/weekly?
- RAG progress/attainment (current and projected) in such a way that those falling behind can be easily identified?
- identify pupils eligible for additional funding (Pupil Premium, etc.)?
- identify pupils with SEN Support and/or with an EHC Plan?
- identify SEN pupils by need type?

Does the system's Provision Mapping facility enable teachers to:

- identify pupils in need of intervention?
- construct intervention groups?
- set targets for interventions?
- set the frequency and duration of interventions and make any necessary adjustments mid-intervention (for instance the adjustment of groups or targets)?
- add pupils (and staff) to interventions?
- evaluate the impact of the interventions against whether the target has been met or not?
- generate reports for parents?

Schools should also reflect on whether the system enables the SENCO to:

- obtain an overview of the interventions in place across classes, year groups and across the school;
- calculate costs for each intervention and for each pupil;
- identify where interventions could be funded through Pupil Premium;
- obtain a whole school evaluation of the impact of the interventions that identifies any that are insufficiently effective.

If a pupil progress web-based system had all of the attributes listed above, I believe that the management of SEN provision could be achieved in such a way that teachers have greater ownership of the intervention and its impact. If the school were assessing and reviewing pupil progress six times a year and using a highly responsive web-based system with a Provision Mapping facility, I would expect the following actions to be easily achievable:

1 Teachers enter assessment data.
2 Teachers identify pupils with stalled or inadequate progress from assessment analysis.
3 At departmental discussion of progress, teachers suggest intervention to re-accelerate progress. If agreed, how it will be staffed is identified.
4 Teachers set SMART intervention targets from formative assessment data.
5 Teachers compose intervention group on system, identify staff responsible, set time and duration and enter target.
6 System calculates cost and identifies any Pupil Premium pupils so that funding can be tracked.
7 At the end of the period of intervention the teacher evaluates the success of the intervention against the target and adds the outcome to the system (Figure 7.1).
8 At the next review of progress the teacher shares the impact of the intervention with the department to inform future practice.
9 The SENCO will construct intervention groups for non-academic interventions and evaluate their impact against target at the end of the intervention period.
10 The system will automatically add all the intervention groups and impact to a whole school analysis spreadsheet (see Figure 7.4 on p. 100).
11 The SENCO uses the spreadsheet to evaluate all the school's interventions, takes action to address any that are inadequate and shares this information widely.

One of the downfalls of such web-based systems is that they rely on the teaching staff to fully understand their responsibility for all pupil progress at all times and to be proactively using the system to set up and evaluate anything they provide that is additional to the school's core offer. They also rely on the linking of support staff to departments, to be deployed by them to deliver the interventions. I believe that in many schools such systems (if used properly and well led) could increase the awareness of teacher responsibility for additional intervention and the pupil's progress when away from the classroom. I also think they can ease the workload of the SENCO by collating information and generating reports swiftly and easily, but I am not so sure that such systems work well unless the SENCO spends considerable time reminding staff of their responsibilities for the creation of intervention groups, and of the need to always update the data.

Whilst I am confident that there are a number of systems available commercially that will meet the needs of most secondary schools (and actually believe that such systems can be preferable to school-based systems), for schools that want to consider an alternative I can propose a relatively simple to use school-based option that would achieve much the same outcome.

School-based Provision Mapping system

Secondary schools tend to employ relatively fewer support staff than primary schools, even though they often provide a range of additional interventions to meet need. The effective secondary schools will be frequently measuring progress and attainment and will be able to identify pupils for intervention. This model recognises that the key areas for academic intervention will generally be in basic skills, English and maths. All departments may provide additional intervention, especially to support revision and coursework. These interventions should be evaluated because the department will want

Group: **Catch Up Reading**

Cost Per Week £50

Edit Group   Group Breakdown

Pupil Name	w/c 15th Sep	w/c 22nd Sep	w/c 29th Sep	w/c 6th Oct	w/c 13th Oct	w/c 20th Oct	w/c 27th Oct	w/c 3rd Nov	w/c 10th Nov	w/c 17th Nov	w/c 24th Nov	w/c 1st Dec	w/c 8th Dec	w/c 15th Dec	w/c 22nd Dec	w/c 29th Dec	w/c 5th Jan	w/c 12th Jan	w/c 19th Jan	w/c 26th Jan	w/c 2nd Feb	w/c 9th Feb	w/c 16th Feb	w/c 23rd Feb	w/c 2nd Mar	Pupil Total	Target Achieved? I am reading confidently in my target book band.
Drummonds, Faiza																								pp	pp	£70.40	☐
Macduff, Sugartya																										£24.66	☐
Ridgley, Tulip																										£24.66	☐
Camposano, Kandasami																										£45.75	☐
Fertorrani, Antonia																										£40.55	☐
Siron, Leigh				pp	pp			pp	pp	pp	pp	pp	pp				pp	pp	pp	pp	pp	pp		pp		£70.40	✓
Washliove, Lutfia																										£70.40	✓
Dearing, Penny																										£70.40	☐
Pavilbey, Huw																										£36.39	☐
Edgell, Rachida																								pp	pp	£24.66	☐
Tea, Rezah				pp	pp			pp	pp	pp	pp	pp	pp	pp			pp	pp	pp	pp	pp	pp		pp	pp	£70.40	✓
Leivers, Alok				pp	pp			pp	pp	pp	pp	pp	pp	pp			pp	pp	pp	pp	pp	pp		pp	pp	£70.40	☐
Oh, Phyllis																										£70.40	☐
Harbron, Roxie																										£70.40	☐
Garltebum, Michaella																										£24.66	✓
Richinga, Ajit				pp	pp			pp	pp	pp	pp	pp	pp	pp			pp	pp	pp	pp	pp	pp		pp	pp	£70.40	✓ ✓
Baker-Lamb, Paula																										£70.40	✓
Cost per pupil	£4.55	£4.55	£4.55	£4.55	£4.55	£4.55		£4.17	£4.17	£3.85	£3.85	£3.85	£3.85	£3.85			£2.94	£2.94	£2.94	£3.13	£3.13	£3.13		£3.13	£3.33		

Figure 7.1 Pupil Asset intervention group

to know whether the intervention is worthwhile. The evaluation will generally centre on whether the pupil still requires the intervention, or the progress has been successfully re-accelerated. Evaluation could, therefore, sometimes be as simple as – the pupil no longer requires the intervention. But in English and maths there may be a need to provide more specific and possibly more intensive intervention to ensure development of basic skills, particularly in lower year groups and for exam year students. Such intervention, where it is delivered by additional staff away from the classroom, should be closely monitored to ensure that targets are being met and determine whether the pupil should be withdrawn from, or remain in, the intervention. Evaluation of intervention would also be required to establish when the graduated response should be increased and the pupil be identified for further assessment and possibly as SEN Support.

If the school wants to adopt a basic model to manage and track such intervention I believe it could introduce a simple form of Provision Mapping that would enable each department to catalogue the provision it makes and measure its effectiveness. As well as the departmental Provision Maps for English and maths, I think that schools that choose this system would also introduce a Provision Map for all the non-academic interventions delivered by the pastoral and SEN team.

In order to successfully adopt this model the school would need to deploy some of its support staff team to the English and maths departments to increase departmental capacity to provide interventions. It would also need to identify one member of staff from English and maths as the Provision Map Leader (PM Leader).

The following actions should then be achievable:

1 Teachers enter assessment data.
2 Teachers identify pupils with stalled or inadequate progress from assessment analysis.
3 At departmental discussion of progress, teachers suggest intervention to re-accelerate progress. If agreed, how it will be staffed from departmental resource is identified.
4 The PM Leader for English and maths departments should record any agreed additional intervention on a departmental Provision Map.
5 The PM Leader for English and maths departments should ensure that teachers have provided SMART targets, timing and frequency details for the interventions before they commence (Figure 7.2).
6 The PM Leader to share the draft departmental Provision Map with the SENCO.
7 The SENCO should oversee the Provision Map for the SEN/AEN department (consulting with teachers on targets where necessary) and link all three maps together into one for each year group.
8 The SENCO should place the year group Provision Map on to the school's shared information system so that all staff are aware of the interventions (and the targets) for pupils' non-academic development.
9 At the end of the period of intervention the PM Leaders will prompt the teachers to evaluate the interventions and record this on the departmental Provision Map(Figure 7.3).
10 The PM Leader will feed back on the impact of the interventions to teachers at the next Pupil Progress Review meeting.
11 The SENCO will evaluate the non-academic interventions that the school provides and place this evaluated Provision Map on the school's shared information system.
12 The SENCO will be responsible for evaluating the impact of all interventions across the school and taking action to address any that is not sufficiently effective.

					Provision Map: English			Start date: Oct 14 end date: December 14

Quality teaching strategies: refer to SEN database for full detail
Must note: JK will need an exit card, PM and ST require work stations occasionally, KLT to have coloured overlay, HA sits at front, PLD and DH work well together, HF and MM need visual support for organisation (task boards are good).

Intervention	Group size	Frequency/ duration/staff	Pupil	Entry data	Intervention target/outcome (SMART)	Exit data	Impact	Proportion target met
Year 7 Comprehension and Exam Technique Group (A)	1:6	3 x 15 x 6 weeks HLTA (tutor time)	HA JK YF ST JL FDP	Entry test score/50 25 21 26 22 24 25	To be able to scan read a text – at least three paragraphs in length – and identify key words and phrases to answer comprehension questions accurately	Exit test score/50		
Year 7 Writing Group (B)	1:6	1 x 30 x 4 weeks (early am) HLTA	KS RC WW AH PM KLT		To be able to understand poetic conventions and how these are used for impact in short poems To be able to identify rhyme and write short rhyming couplets with confidence			
Paired reading	1:1	Daily, x 10 x 8 weeks, HLTA	JK KL MM JP		To use phonic knowledge more securely to segment and blend To re-engage with text Read with expression			

Figure 7.2 Draft English Provision Map

Provision Map: English Start date: Oct 14 end date: December 14

Quality teaching strategies: refer to **SEN** register for full detail
Must note: JK will need an exit card, **PM** and **ST** require work stations occasionally, **KLT** to have coloured overlay, **HA** sits at front, **PLD** and **DH** work well together, **HF** and **MM** need visual support for organisation (task boards are good).

Intervention	Group size	Frequency/duration/staff	Pupil	Entry data	Intervention target/outcome (SMART)	Exit data	Impact	Proportion target met
Year 7 Comprehension and Exam Technique Group (A)	1:6	3 x 15 x 6 weeks HLTA (tutor time)	HA JK YF ST JL FDP	Entry test score/50: 25 21 26 22 24 25	To be able to scan read a text – at least three paragraphs in length – and identify key words and phrases to answer comprehension questions accurately	Exit test score/50: 35 20 30 27 35 40	Positive outcome for all except JK – behaviour an issue. ST/YF need 1:1	5/6
Year 8 Writing Group (B)	1:6	1 x 30 x 4 weeks (early am) HLTA	KS RC WW AH PM KLT		To be able to understand poetic conventions and how these are used for impact in short poems. To be able to identify rhyme and write short rhyming couplets with confidence	Evidence rhyming couplets mastered. AH weak in this area	Good progress. Positive outcome. AH attendance poor	4/6
Paired reading	1:1	Daily, x 10 x 8 weeks, HLTA	JK KL MM JP		To use phonic knowledge more securely to segment and blend. To re-engage with text. Read with expression		Good progress JK better engaged 1:1	4/4

Figure 7.3 Secondary school Provision Map, evaluated

The school should store the advice to teachers on the strategies to use with pupils (particularly the most frequently occurring need types) on an accessible system, such as described in the case study from Wrotham School above. Whatever the school's practice, it should ensure that teachers are made aware of the strategies required for good teaching to achieve good outcomes for the most vulnerable pupils and that interventions should only be considered once such strategies have proven unsuccessful.

The main advantages of the simple school-based system are that departments (especially English and maths departments) retain responsibility for the interventions they are providing which should enhance teacher awareness of them. The main drawback of such a system is that it places the responsibility for monitoring of interventions on the Provision Mapping Leader/SENCO and not directly with the teachers. It also requires some duplication of data – all pupils who access an intervention should have this recorded on the school's MIS (management information system) so that a record can be built up of intervention accessed over time. The simple school-based system will not automatically generate personalised reports for parents, nor will it automatically generate the overview report that many commercial systems do: one that can be used to inform governors of the impact of interventions across the school.

Evaluating interventions

In any system (web-based or school-based) the management of the interventions should include a facility for those delivering the intervention to note attendance and progress or grouping issues. Such documentation could also be used as ongoing communication between those delivering the intervention and the teachers/ SEN staff. Running records of the interventions should be kept and could be entered electronically on to a system that the Provision Mapping Leader and SENCO can monitor. Any teacher needing to review an intervention that they have not delivered should be able to consult such records when considering why targets have been met or not. The format for this record keeping would be school-specific and should be very simple but could include:

- target(s);
- recording of any absence;
- progress notes/comments on grouping, etc.;
- assessment information (if required).

An overview that collates all the evidence of the impact of interventions is a vital source of information for those who want to monitor the school's effectiveness in this area; senior leaders, governors, the local authority and Ofsted. The example from the Pupil Asset system shows the percentage of pupils who met their targets in each intervention (Figure 7.4). Such an analysis tool has many uses. SENCOs would not only share this information with senior leaders and governors, they could also use it to identify any inadequacies and where to prioritise training. In the example provided, Pupil Asset has identified those interventions delivered from Pupil Premium funding (darkest shading) so that the analysis of funding for the school's disadvantaged children

Provision Map Overview	Behaviour Intervention £40 p/h	Revision Counts £30 p/h	Maths Bridge 9 £0 p/h	Boot Camp £0 p/h	Word Play £20 p/h	Advanced Composition £10 p/h	Catch up Maths £30 p/h	Catch up Reading £30 p/h	Write On 7, 8, 9 £30 p/h	Counselling £100 p/h
Year 13	40%	N/A	N/A	67%	N/A	20%	N/A	N/A	N/A	25%
Year 12	50%	N/A	N/A	50%	N/A	50%	N/A	N/A	N/A	0%
Key Stage 5	44%	N/A	N/A	57%	N/A	36		N/A	N/A	20%
Year 11	50%	30%	N/A	67%	50%		N/A	N/A	N/A	50%
Year 10	N/A	50%	N/A	71%	0%	N/A	N/A	N/A	N/A	33%
Key Stage 4	50%	39%	N/A	69%	25%	N/A	N/A	N/A	N/A	40%
Year 9	N/A	N/A	0%	100%	N/A	N/A	N/A	N/A	100%	N/A
Year 8	N/A	N/A	N/A	40%	N/A	N/A	30%	41%	64%	0%
Year 7	N/A	N/A	N/A	0%	N/A	N/A	67%	40%	50%	50%
Key Stage 3	N/A	N/A	0%	43%	N/A	N/A	44%	41%	63%	25%

Group contains Pupil Premium

Figure 7.4 Pupil Asset whole school overview

can be made clear. Armed with this information the GB should be able to make appropriate challenge to the quality of support and impact of funding. For instance, from the example given a GB might question the impact of the very expensive counselling the school is providing. Such information should be provided to governors three times per year.

In both systems, schools could make use of the intervention targets when setting performance appraisal targets for the support staff line managed within each department and should then use the evaluation as evidence of whether targets have been met or not during review meetings.

Sharing Provision Maps with parents in the secondary phase

The SEND Code of Practice states that schools should meet with parents of pupils with SEN at least three times per year and recommends that this is achieved through the regular consultation events. It suggests that the meetings should be between the pupils and their parents and the teacher or tutor who knows the child best, supported by the SENCO. However, it warns that these meetings will take longer than for pupils with no SEN support and should be allocated sufficient time. Secondary schools will need to consider how these arrangements can be made best. There is a fundamental difference between reporting to parents in primary and secondary education. In primary schools consultation is between the parents and the class teacher; in secondary schools the consultation events are generally either held with just the pupil's tutor (where information from all teachers is collated and presented to pupil and parents by the tutor), or the consultation involves a series of brief meetings with all subject teachers. The first scenario probably lends itself better to informing parents about proposed interventions and their targets, as well as any impact of prior intervention; the latter is too fragmented and teachers are too often focused on their own subjects to address more holistic needs and the impact of any additional provision.

However secondary schools address the need to meet with parents, they also need to ensure that parents are kept fully informed about the SEN status of their child and the intervention he/she is receiving. In secondary schools the practice is generally that of sharing individual plans or records that demonstrate the interventions accessed. I have come to accept that the element of primary Provision Mapping that parents find most informative – the ability to set their child's provision in context with that made for all pupils in the class – is not generally possible to achieve in a secondary model, but it may not be necessary. If commercially produced personalised reports are used they must be easy for parents to understand and should clarify the targets the pupil is working towards, both in class and in interventions so that parents can be made aware of how they can help at home. I have included two examples here to show the sort of report I think that parents would find valuable. Figure 7.5 shows a very comprehensive report that includes attendance and behaviour data as well as academic data and the record of the interventions being accessed. Figure 7.6 shows a more intervention-based report with detail of targets and would need to be backed up with other data evidence.

If schools are going to use the usual consultation events to share this information with the parents of pupils with SEN, they may well need to make more opportunities

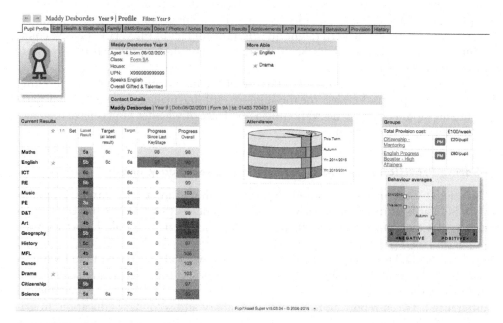

Figure 7.5 Pupil Asset pupil profile

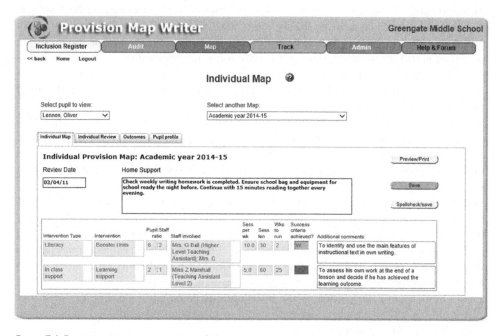

Figure 7.6 Provisionmapwriter: pupil profile

available; most secondary schools do not hold more than one or two consultation events per year. In this case the school will need to report additionally to parents of pupils with SEN. I suggest that the meetings be evenly spaced across the year with the last of the meetings being held at the end of the summer term to support review of intervention across the year and to plan for the new academic year.

Sharing information with other agencies

As well as sharing information with parents and staff, SENCOs will need to provide information of the action the school has taken and the impact of that action with other outside agencies. If a commercial system is used then the school should be able to generate reports that go back over a significant period of time and show all the intervention that a child has accessed, but this will only be of use in demonstrating impact if there is a corresponding record of the outcome of the intervention. If the school is using the simple school-based system described above then anonymised departmental Provision Maps could be used to demonstrate impact over time and the school could use these reports to provide evidence of action and impact when/if requesting statutory assessment. Where the school has adopted a web-based system it should be able to generate an individual Pupil Record, but this will only be of use for the purpose of sharing information with other agencies if it can demonstrate the impact of the intervention the school has provided over time.

I think that whether a commercial, web-based system would be easier and less time-consuming to manage than the school-based system outlined above is debatable. I do believe that a commercial system is generally better perceived by staff in secondary schools who are more used to such automated systems and that such a system almost always collates information for individual pupils more easily. However, I have found the simpler school-based system to be used effectively in some schools and have known teacher awareness of the need for their input to the planning and evaluation of intervention to grow through its use.

Checklist for Provision Mapping in secondary schools

In place in our school?	Yes	No	Needs developing
Some support staff are deployed to the English and maths departments.			
English, maths and SEN Dept. use Provision Maps to manage provision.			
A PM Leader has been appointed in each department who will maintain and evaluate the departmental Provision Map.			
The Provision Maps show the key data including targets and entry and exit data.			
Teachers are involved in intervention target setting and targets are SMART.			
Running records are kept of all intervention.			
Teachers are involved in the evaluation of interventions.			
The school and its governors understand the impact of the interventions.			
Personalised Provision Maps/reports are shared with parents in such a way that they understand the provision their child is receiving and how they can help at home.			

Chapter 8

What should Provision Mapping look like in special schools?

I know that many special schools will have evolved their own systems for tracking pupil progress which will include recording the additional provision made for each of their pupils. They will all be regularly reviewing practice and adjusting provision to ensure it continues to meet need. Despite that, I do believe there is a place for Provision Mapping in special schools which is principally to support the management and review of intervention effectiveness. The school may be recording the personalised intervention provided for each pupil to achieve their outcomes on an Individual Education Plan (IEP), a Provision Plan, a Personal Profile or Pupil Record, and these will be the documents that are shared with parents in review meetings, but such documents are so personalised that information on how effective the interventions are is often difficult to collate. The information may end up sitting in silos within the school. I therefore think that there is just as great a need in special schools as in mainstream schools to evaluate the effectiveness of all the interventions delivered and to determine whether the school is getting value for money. Adopting a system of Provision Mapping could achieve this.

Whilst I do not want schools to have to duplicate any of their actions, I do think that in many special schools a Provision Map can be a useful class management tool and could be used to record the more personalised and individual interventions provided each term on one document, making it easier for a teacher to manage, on a day-to-day basis, than a large number of IEPs. This type of Provision Map could possibly be generated by one of the many commercial packages available. They list what has been provided for each pupil, but I feel that there would be a significant risk that such packages would not be suitably adaptable or allow for the entry of a number of very personalised targets and would therefore be too restrictive.

If the school decides to use a commercial system of pupil progress tracking that incorporates a Provision Mapping facility, it should establish whether it meets the following criteria.

Does the progress tracking system:

- link to the school's Management Information System (MIS) and update pupil information daily?
- identify the teacher who has entered the attainment data?
- RAG progress so that those falling behind can be easily identified?
- identify pupils eligible for additional funding (Pupil Premium, etc.)?
- identify pupils by need type or other school-specific categories?
- generate personalised reports to share with parents?

You should consider whether the system encourages **teachers** to:

- set SMART targets for intervention;
- set the frequency and duration of intervention;
- add pupils (and staff) to interventions;
- evaluate the interventions by prompting them to record whether the target has been met or not;
- generate personalised reports for individual pupils.

The school should also reflect on whether the system will allow it to:

- identify where interventions could be funded through Pupil Premium;
- enter interventions devised by other agencies such as OT, SALT;
- obtain a whole school evaluation of the impact of the interventions that identifies any that are insufficiently effective.

In order to ensure that the system is well used and that the monitoring aspects support school self-evaluation and improvement planning, there must be a member of staff identified to oversee it. In mainstream schools this is usually the SENCO, in special schools I think it should be a senior leader who will co-ordinate the information gathered and be responsible for generating a report on the effectiveness of the interventions for governors, the LA and Ofsted.

Drafting the Provision Map

Having worked with a number of special schools to design a Provision Mapping system to be used by their teachers, I have concluded that the system that works best is broadly similar to the one I use with mainstream schools. It relies on accurate assessment (see Chapter 2) which is analysed and used by teachers to reflect on their practice, as well as to identify those pupils who need something additional and/or different to that which is being provided from the school's core offer. The teacher (primary phase) and/or subject leader (secondary phase) should compose a Provision Map showing the different interventions that are required to meet needs. It should be populated with all the additional interventions accessed by pupils in the class that term, including those interventions recommended or provided by external agencies, and would be reviewed and re-drafted in just the same way as in any mainstream school, at each review of pupil progress.

The cyclical process of Assess, Plan, Do and Review is used in special schools, just as it is in mainstream schools, to determine whether pupils are making progress or not. The action to address any inadequate pupil progress or attainment will always start with assessment. In earlier chapters of this book I have outlined the process for assessing pupils, analysing data and gathering pupil views. Although there are some barriers to measuring pupil progress in special schools – the progress measures for pupils who function below age-related expectations are poorly defined – once the teacher has a clear idea of who is not making good progress, he/she must take action. The teacher should consider strategies and interventions that would be most effective to redress any inadequate progress and the pupils who need to access them. From this the teacher should create a draft version of the class Provision Map for the coming term. In a special school the draft Provision Map for a class would look as it does in Figure 8.1.

Special school class Provision Map

Class: **Date:**

Moderation panel:

Quality first teaching strategies:

Interventions

Pupil	Intervention	Frequency/ staff	Group size	Entry data	Target (SMART)	Exit data	Impact Date:	Target met Y/N

Figure 8.1 Special school Provision Map

© 2016 *Provision Mapping and the SEND Code of Practice*, Anne Massey, Routledge

Date: The Provision Map needs to be dated so that the period of intervention it covers is clear.

Moderation panel: In this version of a Provision Map links to a moderation panel (see Chapter 2) have been incorporated. Assessment of the lowest attaining pupils is more problematic because there are no standardised tests against which to make comparison, and it is therefore important to capture whether assessment accuracy has been challenged. This row on the Provision Map would be populated at the Pupil Progress Review meeting with the names of pupils for whom a moderation panel needs to be convened.

Quality first teaching strategies: I think that the listing of quality first teaching strategies on a special school Provision Map has great merit; the needs of pupils in any school should be addressed primarily through good teaching and all teachers need reminders of 'what works'.

Interventions: The section where intervention is recorded is broadly the same as it is for mainstream schools. The teacher will enter the groups or individuals and interventions proposed for the coming term. Entry or baseline data, where relevant, should be entered alongside pupil names. The teacher should determine the target, which should be **SMART** enough that the teacher will easily be able to ascertain whether it has been met or not at the end of the period of intervention.

- **Specific:** The class teacher will have devised targets that relate to either gaps in learning or to developing skills hitherto undeveloped.
- **Measurable:** This should be clearly evident and, if linked to data, that should be relevant.
- **Achievable** (but also **Aspirational**): Achievable should, in my view, be joined by Aspirational as I would expect that these targets would be used to ensure there is sufficient challenge.
- **Relevant:** The class teacher will have set the targets from a gap analysis, using information from other agencies where relevant and from what is known about the child.
- **Timed:** The targets will remain pertinent for the duration of the Provision Map.

In this section it will also be possible to enter interventions designed and delivered wholly by other agencies. Representatives from these bodies would also contribute to the evaluation at the point of review. However, the teacher will retain responsibility for the Provision Map, a feature that means teachers are even better focused on their responsibility for all pupil achievement. Any intervention funded through Pupil Premium could also be identified here and would support the school's evaluation of the impact of this resource at an individual level.

In an ideal world the teacher would draft the Provision Map from his or her analysis of pupil progress and would share it with senior leaders at the Pupil Progress Review meeting. All at the meeting would discuss the interventions proposed and would agree that proven effective interventions have been selected with appropriate frequency of delivery. The Provision Map would then be agreed and the period of interventions commenced (Figure 8.2). However, in reality not all staff attend Pupil Progress Review meetings this well prepared. In some schools the Provision Map is drafted at the review meeting and in some schools it is drafted following the meeting.

XXXXXX School xxx class Provision Map

Class: **Date: 30.10.2014**

Moderation Panel: MP and JS (both agreed)

Quality first teaching strategies:

Use of the TEACCH approach and strategies within class including the use of the following:

Workstations Individually differentiated 'Work Together' activities Individual schedules/timetables Differentiated use of iPads & computers Daily Attention Autism sessions Letters and Sounds Simplified language Symbol supported communication/learning materials Individual communication systems Write Dance Daily sensory activities within class Sensory room sessions (individual and small group) Count downs Timers Social stories

Interventions:

Pupil	Intervention	Frequency staff	Grp. size	Entry data	Target	Exit data	Impact	Target met Y/N
MP	Speaking & Listening Colourful Semantics	2 x per week	1:1	58% P8	To form 3 part sentences including 'who, doing, what' using colourful semantics			
NW				42% P6				
KL				27% P6				
MP	Reading	2 x per week	1:1	74% P6	To identify ten phonemes from Phase 2 of letters & sounds			
NW	Reading	2 x per week	1:1	37% P7	To identify ten phonemes from Phase 2 of letters & sounds			
KO	Speaking & Listening	3 x per week	1:1	59% P4	Using her communication book KO will communicate what she sees in a book or picture, e.g. I see cow.			

Figure 8.2 Draft special school Provision Map

Maintaining the Provision Map

Whenever it is drafted, once it has been agreed by the leader of Provision Mapping the draft Provision Map becomes a working document. The teaching strategy box may be used by the teacher as a reminder of strategies that have proved to be effective in this class or in other classes, recently or at other times. The teacher can refer to this section of the Provision Map when planning learning activities and when determining groupings etc. It could also be used by members of the SLT when carrying out observations of teaching and learning to determine whether the teaching strategies discussed and advised on during a Pupil Progress Review meeting are in place and fully embedded in daily classroom practice. For example, do pupils regularly refer to the visual timetable in place, thus indicating that it is part of normal classroom practice? Are resources (ear defenders, work stations, etc.) required by individual pupils readily available to and used by them? The information in this box is also of significant importance to any cover teacher, as it provides evidence of the strategies pupils will expect to see in place and will support continuity and consistency if the regular teacher is absent.

In exactly the same way as in mainstream schools, there will need to be a record kept over the course of the intervention to support the teacher's evaluation. It should be easy to use and widely available so that all staff involved with the pupil could access and contribute to it (Figure 8.3). Any reasons why the intervention did not take place or why pupils were absent should also be recorded, as well as any issues that arise around the content of the intervention, the way it is delivered and any issues re timetabling and grouping.

It is not necessary to wait until the end of an intervention period to update a Provision Map. As the term progresses the teacher should update the Provision Map to show changes to teaching strategies where some have proved unsuccessful and others have been added, and changes to groups, frequency and timings of interventions as necessary. The best Provision Maps are those that are regularly scribbled on, adjusted and amended. If a pupil is experiencing a problem in a group, if the timetabling of a group is causing problems, if the frequency of the intervention sessions needs to be increased, adjustments should be made before the end of the intervention period and any changes recorded on the Provision Map.

Evaluating the Provision Map

At the end of the intervention period the Provision Map needs to be evaluated (Figure 8.4). This will be achieved by considering whether the target for the intervention has been met or not. The teacher may need to make reference to the intervention record sheets and/or other datasets such as attendance and behaviour records

If a school is both assessing and reviewing pupil progress six times per year, for the vast majority of interventions the end of the intervention period will coincide with the Pupil Progress Review meetings and the exit data will always be current and relevant. However, for those schools assessing pupils six times per year but only reviewing progress four times per year, the end of the intervention period will not necessarily coincide with the Pupil Progress Review meetings. This has been known to create a dilemma for some schools: when and how to enter the exit data for interventions on the Provision Map? For instance, in a school that assesses and reviews three times per year, an intervention that runs for six weeks will end before the end

Class Oak		Date: Term 4					Teacher: Mrs BD TA JK and FG			
Intervention: Speaking & Listening Colourful Semantics							Timing, frequency and duration:			
Pupils: MP, NW, KL										
Date	10/4	12/4	13/4	18/4	20/4	21/4	25/4	27/4	28/4	5/5	7/5
Absence	MP	X illness		NW	NW	NW		X INSET			

Targets

To form 3 part sentences including 'who, doing, what' using colourful semantics

Observation and progress notes

12/4 No session

13/4 MP very distracted

20/4 NW absence has meant the group has made more progress over this 2 weeks

21/4 KL Good progress and may need further extending

28/4 MP distracted again – think he is unwell

Figure 8.3 Completed special school intervention record sheet

XXXXXX School xxx class Provision Map

Class:

Date: 30.10.2014

Moderation panel: MP and JS (both agreed)

Quality first teaching strategies:
Use of the TEACCH approach and strategies within class including the use of the following:
Workstations Individually differentiated 'Work Together' activities Individual schedules/timetables Differentiated use of iPads & computers Daily Attention Autism sessions Letters and Sounds Simplified language Symbol supported communication/learning materials Individual communication systems Write Dance Daily sensory activities within class Sensory room sessions (individual and small group) Count downs Timers Social stories

Interventions:

Pupil	Intervention	Frequency staff	Grp. size	Entry data	Target	Exit data	Impact	Target met Y/N
MP NW KL	Speaking & Listening Colourful Semantics	2 x per week	1:1	58% P8 42% P6 27% P6	To form 3 part sentences including 'who, doing, what' using colourful semantics	61% P8 46% P6 31% P6	All able to use colourful semantic structure but MP requires further reinforcement. And NW needs reinforcement for verbally complex sentences	Yes
MP	Reading	2 x per week	1:1	74% P6	To identify ten phonemes from Phase 2 of letters & Sounds	76% P6	MP can identify 6 (satpin) phonemes	No
NW	Reading	2 x per week	1:1	37% P7	To identify ten phonemes from Phase 2 of letters & Sounds	58% P7	NW can identify 20 phonemes.	Yes
KO	Speaking & Listening	3 x per week	1:1	59% P4	Using her communication book KO will communicate what she sees in a book or picture, e.g. I see cow.	66% P4	KO has used 'I see' successfully but requires more work to develop her understanding of this.	No

Figure 8.4 Evaluated special school Provision Map

of the school's assessment interval. How should the outcome of the intervention be recorded in such an instance? As I have previously made clear, this system is intended to reduce bureaucracy and so I would advise that the teacher judge whether the target has been met or not at the end of the predetermined period of intervention and record that on the Provision Map at the same time. A true measure of impact is whether any progress gained through the provision of additional intervention is sustained, therefore teachers could record level of attainment (or whether target has been met) at the point of cessation of intervention, and then again at the next assessment point. If the exit data column is split in two and dated, both data could be recorded and the teacher could demonstrate whether any initial gains have been sustained or built on.

Whatever the pattern of assessment and review, before each Pupil Progress Review meeting, all exit data should be entered on to the Provision Map and the impact of the intervention determined by the teacher in preparation for that meeting. A copy of the evaluated Provision Map should be provided for the SLT to consider in the week prior to the Pupil Progress Review meeting. This will enable the school to build up a clear picture of 'what works' and so be able to disseminate that information to other teachers during the Pupil Progress Review meetings and be best placed to consider alternatives to any unsuccessful interventions.

The teacher's review of the impact of interventions needs to be very rigorous in order to ensure that the intervention in place is effective enough. The Ofsted SEN review noted that 'even where assessment was accurate, timely, and identified the appropriate additional support, this did not guarantee that the support would be of good quality'. Further into the review it is reported that:

> Inspectors found that weaker providers did not always evaluate their own provision rigorously enough to identify whether what they were providing for individual pupils was sufficiently effective.
>
> (Ofsted 2010c, p. 40)

If any intervention is considered insufficiently effective the reasons for this should be fully explored by the teacher – did the intervention take place as regularly as intended? Did the intervention design match the needs of the pupils? Was the grouping for the intervention conducive to high levels of engagement? Was the person delivering the intervention sufficiently trained and experienced?

A range of information in addition to the academic assessment data will support the evaluation of impact of intervention. Pupil views should be considered at this point: have any of the pupils commented that the behaviour of other pupils in the intervention group was a barrier to learning? Were there issues of timetabling or grouping? Information can also be gathered from the intervention record sheets: have there been a number of occasions when the intervention did not take place? The teacher should also consider attendance and behaviour data and record any individual or group issues in the impact column so that the evaluation of the intervention is complete. Additional information may need to be gathered from other agencies such as speech and language therapy, physiotherapy, etc. This information will help the teacher to determine the effectiveness of the intervention and would help any school to better understand whether other agency support is giving 'value for money'.

The following case study helps describe the benefits of Provision Mapping in a special school. Ifield School caters for SLD and PMLD pupils and many have a diagnosis of ASD. It is a through school – nursery to post 16 with plans to make provision available beyond 19.

At Ifield School, Provision Mapping is a targeted tool that describes and evaluates all the interventions provided in a given term. The most positive feature of the Provision Maps is that the interventions have a much broader focus than the IEPs (Individual Education Plan) that were used previously. These focus areas can be related to subjects, social development, life skills, sensory programmes, speech and language support, and many more holistic aspects of learning.

The barriers to learning and progress that are addressed through the Provision Mapping system are largely identified at the termly pupil progress meetings that happen at the school. These meetings involve several professionals, usually the class teacher or subject teachers, a member of the speech and language team, and a member of the leadership team who chairs the meeting. Initially, the meetings focus on additional provision that is subject-specific, before identifying where interventions are required for further areas of learning and development.

Prior to the Pupil Progress meetings the class or subject teachers are required to analyse the termly subject data and identify pupils that are consistently making lower quartile progress. The key word here is 'consistently', as the aim of the Provision Map in this instance is to identify the pupils that are not on track to achieve their end-of-year targets, not those whose progress may have temporarily stalled. The class teacher or subject teachers then add the names of the pupils not making expected progress to the Provision Map and the subject area in which their progress needs to be accelerated.

At the pupil progress meeting a professional discussion takes place about the intervention that will have the most impact on pupil progress in this subject area. The main reason for having several professionals involved in this discussion is to ensure that all views are represented. Once a target is agreed upon it is added to the Provision Map along with further information, including who will provide the intervention and the frequency with which it will be delivered.

More recently class and subject teachers have also been required to look for pupils consistently making upper quartile progress. This has become an important feature in ensuring that Provision Maps are not just seen within the school as a tool to support 'lower-achieving' learners, but also a way of providing additional challenge for those that require it. On the Provision Map, these pupils can be highlighted as requiring an intervention that could range from more challenging homework to weekly inclusion in another school. This shows that the Provision Map is being used as a tool for the school's inclusion information.

Once the subject-specific interventions have been recorded on the Provision Map, the broader areas of learning are focused on. This is largely why the school considers it important to have a member of the speech and language team present at the meetings; they are able to provide information on the interventions that are required for a range of language and social development issues. These interventions have often been pre-determined by the speech and language team, but are recorded on the Provision Map in the same way, with a clear target, lead person and frequency of the provision. Class teachers are required to discuss in advance any further interventions with professionals who may not be present at the Pupil Progress meeting but need to contribute. An example of this would be a physiotherapy programme initiated by occupational therapists.

Once the pupil progress meeting is finished, the class teacher should have a Provision Map that documents every intervention that will be provided for that class over the coming term. This information is then shared with the class support team who will often be involved in leading the interventions. It is important that those leading the interventions report back regularly to the class teacher, as the Provision Maps are evaluated at the end of each term. The evaluation summarises whether the intervention target has been achieved and, as a result, whether the intervention can be terminated or whether it needs to continue with a revised target. The reason for the school operating this system on a termly basis is that it provides enough time for interventions to take effect, but not so much time that they become 'stale' or lose impetus. It is unusual for an intervention to continue for longer than two terms without being achieved or altered, as this would suggest it is not having sufficient effect and another intervention may be necessary.

The school has found Provision Mapping extremely useful; in many cases the process has accelerated the progress of pupils in different areas. In other instances it provides evidence that the action the school is taking to offer pupils the best opportunity to make progress is effective. The evaluation of the Provision Maps across the school provides quantitative evidence of the effectiveness of interventions which can, in turn, be used to provide evidence of impact to the governing body.

(Neil Dipple, Assistant Director for Achievement,
Ifield Special School, Gravesend, Kent)

Sharing Provision Maps with parents

The sharing of Provision Maps with parents is probably the only area of the Provision Mapping system where special schools would differ significantly from mainstream schools. Special schools must consult with parents with the same regularity as mainstream schools and many do so far more frequently. However, the parents of pupils in special schools do not need to see the provision their child is accessing in context with other pupils, as all will have individual, specific needs and require very different intervention. Thus, although there should be regular parent consultation opportunities to share information about the interventions as recommended in the SEND Code of Practice, I do not believe it is necessary to share the Provision Map with parents if the school has another method of recording information and demonstrating to parents that additional intervention is successful. Any school using a commercial Provision Mapping system may find that the individual reports generated by the system are extremely helpful and avoid too much duplication. However, any school using a school-based system could personalise the Provision Map and demonstrate on one document all the intervention a single pupil receives, as in Figure 8.5.

In whatever format information is shared with parents they must be able to understand the targets and how they can help their child at home. The best example I have of such practice is at Ridge View Special School in Kent. The school has appointed a Personalised Interventions Manager (PIM) to oversee all the intensive intervention it

Ifield School individual Provision Map

Class: **Date:**

Moderation panel:

Quality first teaching strategies: differentiated work appropriate for individual needs, 1:1 TA support, Learning through sensory and exploratory activities.

Interventions

Pupil	Intervention	Frequency/ staff	Group size	Entry data	Target (SMART)	Exit data	Tmpact date:	Target met Y/N
XXXX	Swing room session	15 minutes daily/ 2 staff	2 pupils	English (Reading)- 44% of P6	To increase focus during lessons			
	TAC PAC massage/ Proprioception	30 minutes weekly/ 2 staff	2 pupils	English (Writing)- 9% of P5	To develop levels of awareness and intentional communication			
	Sensory diet	5 minutes, 3 times daily/ 1 staff	1 pupil	English (Listening)- 7% of P6	To develop focus and reduce physically challenging behaviours			
	Hydrotherapy session	1 hour weekly/ 2 staff	2 pupils	English (Speaking)- 26% of P5	To develop body awareness. To practise getting dressed/ undressed			
	Write dance	30 minutes weekly/ 2 staff	2 pupils	Maths (Number)- 52% of P5 Maths (SSM)- 73% of P5 Maths (U&A)- 71% of P5	To develop fine and gross motor skills			

Speech therapy/ Intensive interaction	20 minutes weekly/ 2 staff	1 pupil	To show engagement with an adult during interaction activities	
Workstation	3 minutes, 3 times daily/ 1 staff	1 pupil	To increase attention and focus in lesson times	
Independent eating skills	30 minutes daily/ 1 staff	1 pupil	To use PECs to make food choices To eat using a spoon	
Communication and interaction time	15 minutes, 2 times daily/ 1 staff	1 pupil	To make a choice from 2 options using PECs symbols	
Supervised play	35 minutes daily/ 1 staff	1 pupil	To increase interaction with others during play times	
Sensory room	30 minutes weekly/ 2 staff	2 pupils	To develop focus and reduce physically challenging behaviours	

Figure 8.5 Ifield School individual Provision Map

delivers. From their excellent assessment practice (see Chapter 2) they identify pupils who require intensive intervention and meet with parents of those pupils prior to the start of the intervention to discuss and agree outcomes and targets. The discussion also includes how the parents can help at home. Some of this intervention is funded through Pupil Premium, but not all. Over the course of the intervention period the PIM keeps in touch with parents and then meets with them again to review the impact at the end. The school reports that this level of parental involvement has contributed to significant improvement in the success of their interventions and improved parental confidence exponentially.

Reporting the impact of interventions

All schools will want to know how effective their interventions are across the school and will want to collate this information into an easy to understand format for governors, the LA and Ofsted to use when reviewing the impact of the school's work. I believe that if the Provision Maps are properly evaluated the senior leader who manages Provision Mapping should be able to collate the information into one document. This document should show the proportion of pupils in each year group who have achieved the intervention target set for that period (Figure 8.6). It would help the school to identify any areas of weakness and would provide a vehicle for governor challenge – 'why are some interventions apparently more effective in some year groups than others?' If properly annotated it would also allow the identification of Pupil Premium spending on intervention – all the boxes highlighted will have been funded through Pupil Premium – thus providing a very transparent overview.

Evaluation of impact of interventions Date: September–December 2014																	
Proportion reaching targets	SALT	Language	Physio	1:1 reading	Phonics	Literacy support group 1 & 2	Writing support	Writing extension	Reading extension	Lit. booster	Comprehension group	Numeracy group	Numicon	Extension maths	Number booster	Lego therapy	Therapeutic play
Year R	7/8		5/5														
Class 1	6/8	6/8	8/8										8/8			3/3	
Class 2	2/2		2/3		2/2							2/2	5/5			3/3	
KS 1																	
Class 3	2/5	5/5		4/4	3/3												
Class 4	5/5	2/3	4/4		7/7								7/7			2/3	
Class 5		1/2	2/2		2/2	4/4											
Class 6	3/6		3/3	6/6		6/6		1/1	4/4				4/4			1/3	
KS2																	

Figure 8.6 Overview of impact of interventions in a special school

Checklist for Provision Mapping in special schools

In place in our school?	Yes	No	Needs developing
Provision Maps, drafted by teachers, showing the key data including targets and entry and exit data.			
SMART intervention targets.			
Provision Maps evaluated by class teachers.			
Intervention record sheets used to record key data for each intervention and as a simple system for sharing information between TA and teacher.			
Intervention information shared with parents in such a way that they understand the provision their child is receiving and how they can help at home.			
Information collated and shared with governors.			

Chapter 9

Lastly . . .

The school-based systems that I have described in this book have been tried and tested in primary, secondary and special schools where teachers, SENCOs and headteachers report that they have found the proposals to be sensible, manageable and effective in improving outcomes and improving communication with parents. The commercial systems that I have referred to are constantly evolving and improving and I have high hopes that there will soon be a Provision Mapping facility embedded in all pupil progress tracking systems. I believe that each and every school needs to find a user-friendly, time-efficient method of establishing whether the additional intervention that it is providing is working in the way it is intended to. Schools should not have to spend too long on managing this system; instead schools should have a system that works so smoothly and automatically that – as in that old analogy – they can spend more time feeding the pig than measuring it!

You may have some or all of the elements of this system already in place in your school and will only need to consider and slightly adapt your practice to ensure that you are getting the maximum impact from all that you do. Alternatively you may have to start afresh; you may have to introduce Provision Maps to your staff members, governors, and to the parents of your pupils. Governors may never have had a role in challenging the impact of the interventions you provide and may need support and guidance to make that level of challenge appropriately. Teachers may need intensive support and training that will help them fully understand their responsibility for pupil progress in interventions and their role in Provision Mapping. SENCOs may need support in how to evaluate the impact of the interventions in place across the school.

The cycle of actions that make up the 'graduated approach' should run through the course of a year with no real definition of start or end and with little need for adjustment. The use of Provision Mapping will ensure that the 'graduated approach' is well managed but there are some factors that would limit its effectiveness.

In only two schools with which I have worked has this system not been effective and in both of those schools the system was not well led. I am afraid this system will not work in the way it is intended to if it is introduced to a school by the SENCO, but not backed by the leadership team and headteacher. As it is dependent upon links to the performance management cycle, the governor meeting cycle and the whole school timetable, it must be strongly led to ensure that all stages of the system are effective. Staff members must be helped to adhere to the sometimes challenging demands of the timescale and to become proficient at data analysis and SMART target-setting, but they must also be held to account if they do not. This would need the endorsement of the headteacher to ensure it has the necessary impact. Governors need support and direction to enable them to ask the right questions and to seek information of the highest quality, and will rely on the headteacher or senior leaders for this. Self-evaluation and school development planning will be enhanced by this system as will any conversation about progress, attainment and intervention with Ofsted during inspection. For any school to be fully effective all classroom teaching must be at least good; where it is less than good this system will support a headteacher in securing rapid and sustainable improvement in the quality of teaching across the school.

The first action that I recommend schools take in introducing this system to their school is to establish a school calendar at the start of the year with all aspects of this system clearly laid out (Figure 9.1). Most schools will already have such a calendar. If you do not, this calendar has been created for a school that intends to assess and review six times per year. If you were to choose to assess and/or review less frequently you would need to adjust the calendar accordingly. It is linked to the proposed three-year cycle for moderation, the performance management cycle, parent consultation and governing body meetings. Once an annual calendar has been agreed it should be published to all staff members, so that they are fully prepared for every stage of the system and can plan their activities accordingly. It should be published to governors so that they can arrange their formal and informal visits, the headteacher performance management target-setting and review meetings, and their governing body meeting cycle. These can then be aligned with times when the school will be able to provide it with the most up-to-date information on the percentage of pupils on track to achieve their targets, the progress being made by vulnerable groups (including pupils eligible for Pupil Premium) and the impact of the most recently delivered interventions.

Parents in mainstream schools who have had long experience of SEN provision may feel anxious about changes to the SEND Code of Practice and will need careful support to understand them. If mainstream schools adopt the system of Provision Mapping, parents will become better informed by class teachers at parent consultation meetings about the progress their child is making and the intervention in place to help accelerate it where necessary, and should have less need to meet with the SENCO to discuss progress or intervention. Preparation for statutory assessment should be aided by the constant review of what has worked for a pupil and the evaluative Provision Maps can provide valuable evidence with no need for alteration save for anonymisation. In special schools where this system is adopted there is opportunity for a better analysis of the impact of all the additional intervention that the school offers, better challenge from governors, better identification of how Pupil Premium is being used and to what effect, and teachers should be better able to manage the number and range of interventions provided.

Despite all the recent changes to the curriculum, assessment and SEN, nothing of the system of Provision Mapping I wrote about previously has radically altered, gone out of date or become redundant. Irrespective of national or local policy, schools will always need to know how well their pupils are doing, who needs additional support, what needs to be done to help them make better progress and whether it has worked. Schools will always need to share information with governing bodies,

2014/15	Term 1	Term 2	Term 3	Term 4	Term 5	Term 6
Week 1	Baseline assessment if necessary	Parent consultation	Moderation P Scales (mainstream)	Parent consultation and questionnaire		Moderation history
Week 2		Performance management target-setting	Professional development meeting	Performance management review meeting Pupil questionnaire		Performance management review meeting
Week 3	Professional development meeting	Moderation Computing	Observations	Govenors' meeting	Moderation maths	
Week 4	Moderation: reading	Governors' meeting	Moderation writing	Moderation science	Observations	Assessment Data analysis Pupil views Evaluate Provision Map
Week 5	Observations		Assessment Data analysis Pupil views Evaluate Provision Map	Assessment Data analysis Pupil views Evaluate Provision Map		Progress Review (transition) Draft Provision Map Report to/meet parents
Week 6			Progress Review Draft Provision Map	Progress Review Draft Provision Map	Assessment Data analysis Pupil views Evaluate Provision Map	Gov meeting
Week 7	Assessment Data analysis Pupil views Evaluate Provision Map	Assessment Data analysis Pupil views Evaluate Provision Map			Progress Review Draft Provision Map	
Week 8	Progress Review Draft Provision Map	Progress Review Draft Provision Map				

Figure 9.1 Annual school Provision Mapping calendar

parents and outside agencies, and schools will always need to self-evaluate and plan for further development.

Despite all the challenges schools face in trying to navigate their way through the endless series of complex policy changes it is vital that they maintain their core values: remembering that children are all different and that our job as teachers is to make sure that they all enjoy and engage in school life in its broadest sense as well as make good progress. Whether your school is an academy, a free school, an independent or a maintained school, whether it is a primary, secondary or special school, whether you choose to use a school-based system or a commercial web-based system, this system should be central to all that you do to improve outcomes for pupils, and right at the very heart of it sits the Provision Map itself, a tool for collecting and collating all the information.

Bibliography

AAIA Assessment Systems for the Future Conference (2006) aaia.org.uk, accessed 6 January 2015.

Ainscow, M. (ed.) (1991) *Effective Schools for All*. London: Fulton.

Ainscow, M. (1999) *Understanding the Development of Inclusive Schools*. London: Routledge Falmer.

Ainscow, M. (2005a) 'From special education to effective schools for all'. Keynote presentation at the International Special Education Conference, Glasgow, Scotland.

Ainscow, M. (2005b) 'Developing inclusive education systems: what are the levers for change?'. *Journal of Educational Change* 6(2).

Ainscow, M. and Farrell, P. (2003) *Using Research to Encourage the Development of Inclusive Practices: Making Special Education Inclusive*. London: Fulton.

Ainscow, M. and Miles, S. (2008) 'Making education for all inclusive: where next?'. University of Manchester, UK Paper prepared for *Prospects*, February.

Ainscow, M., Booth, T., Dyson, A. with Farrell, P., Frankham, J., Gallanaugh, F., Howes, A. and Smith, R. (2006) *Improving Schools, Developing Inclusion*. London: Routledge.

Allen, J. (2003) 'Productive pedagogies and the challenge of inclusion'. *British Journal of Special Education* 30(4): 175–179.

Altrichter, H., Feldman, A., Posch, P. and Somekh, B. (2000) *Teachers Investigate Their Work*. London and New York: Routledge.

Assessment Reform Group (1999) *Assessment for Learning: Beyond the Black Box*. Cambridge: University of Cambridge School of Education.

Bamburg, J. (1994) Excerpted from the NCREL monograph, *Raising Expectations to Improve Student Learning*. NCREL.

Beckhard, R. (1969) *Organization Development: Strategies and Models*. Reading, MA: Addison-Wesley.

Black, P. (1998). *Testing: Friend or Foe? Theory and Practice of Assessment and Testing*. London: Falmer Press.

Black, P. and Wiliam, D. (1998). 'Assessment and classroom learning'. *Assessment in Education* 5: 7–74.

Black, P., Gardner, J. and Wiliam, D. (2008) Joint Memorandum on Reliability of Assessments. Submitted to the Children, Schools and Families Committee. In *Testing and Assessment. Third Report of Session 2007–2008*. Norwich: Stationery Office.

Black Hawkins, K., Florian, L. and Rouse, M. (2007) *Achievement and Inclusion in Schools*. London and New York: Routledge.

Blatchford, P., Bassett, P., Brown, P., Martin, C., Russell, A. and Webster, R. (2009) *Deployment and Impact of Support Staff Project*. London: Institute of Education, University of London.

Booth, T. (1999) *From Special Needs Education to Education for All: A Discussion Document*. Paris: UNESCO.

Booth, T. and Ainscow, M. (eds) (1998) *From Them to Us: An International Study of Inclusion in Education*. London: Routledge.

Booth, T. and Ainscow, M. (revised 2002) *Index for Inclusion*. Bristol: Centre for Studies on Inclusive Education.

Brooks, G. (2013) *What Works for Children and Young People with Literacy Difficulties? The Effectiveness of Intervention Schemes* (4th edn). London: The Dyslexia-SpLD Trust.

CASPA Newsletter (2015) www.caspaonline.co.uk.

Corbett, J. (2001) *Supporting Inclusive Education: A Connective Pedagogy*. London: Routledge Falmer.

Costa, A.L. and Kallick, B. (1993) 'Through the lens of a critical friend'. *Educational Leadership* 51(2): 50.

DCSF (2004) *Intensifying Support Programme*. London: Stationery Office.

DCSF (2007) *Primary National Strategy: Pupil Progress Meetings, Prompts and Guidance*. London: Stationery Office.

DCSF (2009a) *Progression Guidance*. DCSF ref: 00553-2009BKT-EN.

DCSF (2009b) *Deployment and Impact of Support Staff in Schools*. DCSF-RR148/DCSF-RB148.

Delamont, S. (2002) *Fieldwork in Educational Settings: Methods, Pitfalls and Perspectives*. London and New York: Routledge.

DfE (2010) *The Importance of Teaching*. The Schools White Paper 2010 ref: CM 7980.

DfE (2011a) *Achievement for All National Evaluation*. Final Report. DFE Ref: RR176, November.

DfE (2011b) *Support and Aspiration: A New Approach to Special Educational Needs and Disability: A Consultation*. Norwich: Stationery Office.

DfE (2011c) *Teachers' Standards in England from 2012*. DfE ref: V1.0 0711.

DfE (2014a) *Assessment Principles*. April 2014.

DfE (2014b) *Performance Descriptors for Use in Key Stage 1 and 2 Statutory Teacher Assessment for 2015/2016. A Consultation*. October 2014.

DfE (2015) *Special Educational Needs and Disability Code of Practice: 0 to 25 years*. DfE ref. DFE-00205-2013

DfES (2003) *Raising Standards and Tackling Workload: A National Agreement*. DfES ref: 0172 2003.

DfES (2004a) *Removing Barriers to Achievement*. DfES ref: 0117/2004D35/PPSTERL/0804/83.

DfES (2004b) *Every Child Matters*. DfES ref: 0786/2004.

DfES (2006) *Effective Leadership: Ensuring the Progress of Pupils with SEN and/or Disabilities*. London: Stationery Office.

DfES (2007) *Making Great Progress: Schools with Outstanding Rates of Progression in Key Stage 2*. DfES ref: 00443-2007BKT-EN.

DfES/DCSF (2009) *The Improving Schools Programme Handbook*. DCSF ref: 00314-2009BKT-EN.

Durrant, J. and Holden, G. (2006) *Teachers Leading Change: Doing Research for School Improvement*. London: Paul Chapman.

European Agency for Special Needs and Inclusive Education (2008) www.european-agency.org/agency-projects/assessment-resource-guide/documents/2008/11/Laevers.pdf.

Ekins, A. and Grimes, P. (2009) *Inclusion: Developing an Effective Whole School Approach*. New York: McGraw-Hill.

Frederickson, N. and Cline, T. (2006) *Special Educational Needs, Inclusion and Diversity: A Textbook*. Milton Keynes: Open University Press.

Fullan, M. (ed.) (1993) *The Challenge of School Change: A Collection of Articles*. Arlington, IL: IRI/SkyLight Training and Publishing.

Fullan, M. (2003) *Change Forces with a Vengeance*. London: Routledge Falmer.

Gronn, P. (2003) *The New Work of Educational Leaders: Changing Leadership Practice in an Era of School Reform.* London: Sage.

Gross, J. (2008) *Beating Bureaucracy in Special Educational Needs.* London and New York: Routledge and NASEN.

Gross, J. and White, A. (2003) *Special Educational Needs and School Improvement.* London: Fulton.

Hanko, G. (1999) *Increasing Competence through Collaborative Problem Solving.* London: Fulton.

Hart, S. (1996) *Beyond Special Needs: Enhancing Children's Learning Through Innovative Thinking.* London: Paul Chapman.

Hart, S., Dixon, A., Drummond, M.J., McIntyre, D. with Brach, N., Conway, C., Madigan, N., Marshall, J., Peacock, A., Reay, A., Tahibet, Y., Worrall, N. and Yarker, P. (2004) *Learning without Limits.* Milton Keynes: Open University Press, McGraw-Hill Education.

Higgins, S., Kokotsaki, D. and Coe, R. (2011) *Toolkit of Strategies to Improve Learning: Summary for Schools Spending the Pupil Premium.* Sutton Trust, Centre for Evaluation and Monitoring, May.

Hopkins, D. (2007) *Every School a Great School.* Milton Keynes: Open University Press, McGraw-Hill Education.

Howes, A., Davies, S.M.B. and Fox, S. (2009) *Improving the Context for Inclusion: Personalising Teacher Development through Collaborative Action Research.* London and New York: Routledge.

Kuglemass, J.W. (2004) *The Inclusive School: Sustaining Equity and Standards.* New York: Teachers College Press.

Lamb, B. (2009) *SEN and Parental Confidence.* London: Crown Copyright.

MacBeath, J. (2006*)* 'School inspection and self-evaluation: working with the new relationship'. *Improving Schools* 10(199): 199–200.

MacBeath, J. (2009) 'Border crossings'. *Improving Schools* 12(1): 81–92.

Mansell, W., James, M. and the Assessment Reform Group (2009) *Assessment in Schools. Fit for Purpose? A Commentary by the Teaching and Learning Research Programme.* London: Economic and Social Research Council, Teaching and Learning Research Programme.

Massey, A. (2013) *Provision Mapping: Improving Outcomes in Primary Schools.* London: Routledge.

Meadmore, D. (2001) 'The pursuit of standards: simply managing education?' *International Journal of Inclusive Education* 5(4): 353–365, available online at: http://ejournals.ebsco.com/direct.asp?ArticleID=8G35PHMEKEHF2TWATULX (accessed 20 August 2009).

Mitchell, D. (2008) *What Really Works in Special and Inclusive Education: Using Evidence-based Teaching Strategies.* London and New York: Routledge.

nasen (2014) *Everybody Included: The SEN Code of Practice Explained.* nasen website.

Ofsted (2004a) *A New Relationship with Schools.* Office for Standards in Education.

Ofsted (2004b) *Special Educational Needs and Disability, Towards Inclusive Schools.* Office for Standards in Education.

Ofsted (2010a) *Special Educational Needs and/or Disabilities in Mainstream Schools: A Briefing Paper for Section 5 Inspectors.* Office for Standards in Education.

Ofsted (2010b) *Workforce Reform in Schools: Has It Made a Difference?* Office for Standards in Education.

Ofsted (2010c) *Special Educational Needs and Disability Review: A Statement Is Not Enough.* Office for Standards in Education. ref: 090221.

Ofsted (2011) *Subsidiary Guidance: Supporting the Inspection of Maintained Schools and Academies from January 2012.* Office for Standards in Education. ref: 110166.

Ofsted (2012) *The Evaluation Schedule for the Inspection of Maintained Schools and Academies from January 2012.* Office for Standards in Education. ref: 090098.

Ofsted (2015, January) *School Inspection Handbook*. Office for Standards in Education. ref: 120101, available online at: www.ofsted.gov.uk/resources/120101.

Ofsted (2015, June) *School Inspection Handbook*. Office for Standards in Education, ref: 15006.

Qualifications and Curriculum Authority (2009) *Research into Marking Quality: Studies to Inform Future Work on National Curriculum Assessment*. London: QCA.

Randall, M. and Thornton, B. (2001) *Advising and Supporting Teachers*. Cambridge: Cambridge University Press.

Robson, C. (2002) *Real World Research* (2nd edn). Oxford: Blackwell.

Rouse, M. and Florian, L. (2006) 'Inclusion and achievement: student achievement in secondary schools with higher and lower proportions of pupils designated as having special educational needs'. *International Journal of Inclusive Education* 10(6): 481–494.

SEND Code of Practice [2015] *Special Educational Needs and Disability Code of Practice: 0 to 25 Years*. DfE ref: DFE-00205-2013.

TLRP (Teaching and Learning Research Programme) (2009), available online at www.tlrp.org/pub/documents/assessment.pdf.

UNESCO (1994) *The Salamanca Statement and Framework for Action on Special Needs Education*. Madrid: UNESCO.

UNICEF (2007) 'Child poverty in perspective: an overview of child well-being in rich countries'. *Innocenti Report Card 7*, UNICEF Innocenti Research Centre, Florence.

West, M., Ainscow, M. and Stanford, J. (2005) 'Sustaining improvement in schools in challenging circumstances: a study of successful practice'. *School Leadership & Management* 25(1): 77–93.

Whitehead, J. and McNiff, J. (2006) *Action Research: Living Theory*. London: Sage.

Wrigley, T. (2006) *Another School Is Possible*. London: Bookmarks Publications and Trentham Books.

Index